Guardsman Philip W... the Falklands War; t... was to change his l... somehow Philip was left for dead on the mountain, and when he came to, the British contingent had totally disappeared. It was to take Philip seven weeks to find his way back to civilization – a time of atrocious blizzards, scant food and the company of dead Argentinian soldiers – but his nightmare was only just beginning. In his absence his parents had been informed of his death and a memorial service had been held in his honour. When the press would not stop distorting the facts his joyful return soon turned sour, and life in the Army was quickly to prove as tough, leaving Philip feeling victimised and isolated.

Irrevocably scarred by his experiences on the Falklands and their aftermath, not to mention his hostile treatment by the media, at last Philip tells his version of what happened to him and the real reasons behind his subsequent rejection of both the Army and a 'normal' civilian life.

Novelist M. S. Power approached Philip after reading a magazine article on him. *Summer Soldier* is the outcome of their meeting; often provocative, it is a searing portrait of someone who finds it impossible to fit in, a story of utterly compulsive reading.

M. S. Power lives in Scotland and has written six novels, including *The Crucifixion of Septimus Roach*.

SUMMER SOLDIER

Philip Williams
with
M. S. Power

BLOOMSBURY

All rights reserved: no part of this publication may be reproduced,
stored in a retrieval system, or transmitted in any form or by any
means, electronic, mechanical, photocopying or otherwise, without
the prior written permission of the publisher.

First published in Great Britain 1990

Copyright © Philip Williams and M. S. Power 1990

Bloomsbury Publishing Ltd, 2 Soho Square, London W1V 5DE

A CIP catalogue record for this book is available
from the British Library

ISBN 0 7475 0598 5

10 9 8 7 6 5 4 3 2 1

Photoset by Rowland Phototypesetting Ltd,
Bury St Edmunds, Suffolk
Printed and bound in Great Britain by
Richard Clay Ltd, Bungay, Suffolk

For my Dad, who tried to understand.

And to the few who have freed their minds from the motivations of power and authority which demand war as a civilised policy.

LIST OF ILLUSTRATIONS

Philip in his Scots Guards uniform, shortly after enlisting. (Times Newspapers Ltd)

Outside the Falklands army field hospital, supported by nurses Lieutenant Corporal Liz Jones and Captain Judy Gorrod, 3 August 1982. (Press Association)

Reunited with Mam and Dad, 10 August 1982. (Press Association)

With Alison, the same day. (Press Association)

A staged photograph of Philip, just after his return. (Press Association)

The Williams family: (l–r) Angela, Dad, Karen, Alison, Philip, Gareth, Mam, and Cherith. (Press Association)

During the filming of *Resurrection*, with David Thewlis, the actor who played Philip. (Philip Williams)

PROLOGUE

To begin with, this isn't *really* a diary, but it would have been if I had one — a diary, I mean. Instead, what I've got is loads and loads of scraps of paper and envelopes and things which I'm going to have to try and sort out as I go along. I've even got about eighteen pages of that beige-coloured crap paper that they make that unfortunate puppy chase, and I can tell you from experience it's not half as tough as they say it is when you try to write on it, and if it gets wet then you're in dire trouble.

Now, I *know* anyone who joins the army can't be all that bright, but I don't want you to think I'm dumb. I don't think I am. Not brilliant or anything, but not a complete dickhead either. However, I won't be giving you lovely descriptions of things because, believe me, there's nothing lovely about war. I'm just going to tell you what happened to me and then you can make up your own minds.

And another thing, something you might not be used to: I'm going to tell you the truth, because I know if I lie I'll only be kidding myself and it won't make a damn bit of difference to you one way or the other. Mind you, you've only got my word for this and, since I'll probably be contradicting a lot that's been written already, I know I'm on a hiding to nothing, as they say. So all I *can* do is tell you the truth and let you make up your own minds.

In the end you probably won't like me, and I'll be sorry about that. But the thing is that I like myself now, and that's pretty important. Well, maybe I don't exactly like myself but I can live with myself, and not be ashamed of anything I did, and look everyone in the eye, and that's a good feeling, believe me.

BOOK ONE

ONE

It'd be handy if I could grab your sympathy right at the beginning by telling you all about my deprived child-hood, and about how I was a real little angel who was misunderstood, and how my great talents were suppressed. But I can't. I was a right little sod, cheeky as hell, and always getting into trouble of one sort or another; nothing too serious, mind, just petty stuff. And I wasn't deprived of anything. My Dad has his own haulage business, and he does well, so there was always enough money about. He works bloody hard, out all hours of the day and night, so I didn't see that much of him, which was just as well since I'd probably have had more beltings than I did, and maybe deserved them too.

My Mam is usually pretty quiet, keeping herself to herself. She works in a home for elderly people. She's very proud of her house, which is always as clean as a whistle, inside and out. There's even a sign up telling you not to smoke, so if you're dying for a fag you have to go outside.

I've got three sisters and a little brother, and that's

really all you need to know about my family for now. Just a very ordinary family really, getting on with their lives and not bothering anyone, and not wanting to be bothered either.

I didn't take much to school. I played truant when I could, which was quite often, taking off up the moors and spending the day there by myself, or doing a bit of fishing or poaching. Poaching was best since anything I caught tasted that much better as there'd been a bit of risk getting it.

I won't say my teachers were afraid of me or anything stupid like that, but they didn't seem to bother really whether I was in class or not. I expect they were quite glad when I wasn't there, since it can't have been very rewarding for them trying to teach someone like me who wouldn't pay attention, and who didn't give a monkey's what they were saying. Why should I care if some old king burnt his buns or had dealings with a goddamn spider or decapitated his wives when he got sick of them? So they pretty well ignored me, leaving me to daydream as much as I wanted, and that's what I usually did, gazing out of the window, miles away, having my own fantastic adventures, and waiting for the time to come when I could get out of the classroom.

Of course Mam and Dad worried about the way I was behaving. Well, Mam did, anyway, but I'll tell you more about that later. Enough to say that I paid no heed, thinking I knew best as usual.

So I left school having learned only the basics. At least I could write and read and add up a bit, which is more than can be said for some of the yobs who went faithfully to school every day. Funnily enough, to this day I've never found anyone who found algebra useful to them when looking for a job on the building site or in a factory.

Speaking of work, to put it mildly work about Lancaster is pretty limited. All I could get was this godawful job in a chicken factory. That was really bad. Just thinking about the stink of raw chicken that hit me every morning still makes me want to puke. If you've ever had to clean out a chicken you'll know what I'm talking about, and I was supposed to do hundreds of the buggers every day. Anyway, *that* didn't last long, I can tell you. Fuck this for a lark, I thought one day, and pissed off. It was ages before I could bring myself to eat chicken again.

Next I got a job labouring on a farm; an agricultural specialist, I called it for a laugh when anyone asked me what I was up to. To begin with it was pretty good. I was outdoors, and I quite liked working with the animals since they didn't keep needling me. But it was such pointless kind of work, the sort that wasn't going to get *me* anywhere although it was getting the farmer anywhere he wanted in his smart, flashy Jaguar. Anyway, I didn't want to be shovelling cow shit for the rest of my life, so I chucked that job in too.

Then came a stint in a cotton mill that lasted about six weeks. All I did there was take the rolls of woven material off the looms and lug them to some other place to be sampled. Really menial it was, and boring.

After that I worked at an indoor market, heaving stuff about again, unloading lorries and carrying the fruit and veg into the market. I didn't *want* to do any of those jobs. I only took them to get my parents off my back, so that I'd have a bit of peace when I went home, and my Dad wouldn't always be going on about having to feed me while I did nothing. I can't remember how long I was working in the market. Not long, though. But long enough as far as I was concerned. Too bloody long in fact.

When I packed that in I started regular trips to the Job Centre to see what gems they had to offer. Not a lot, I can tell you. Nothing, if you had no qualifications or experience like me. So in the end I stopped looking, just pretending to my Mam that I was going down again to have another go, but usually bumming off to Lancaster to see my mates who were out of work too, and as cheesed off as myself.

In the end, of course, my parents got fed up with me for being nothing but a layabout as they put it. To tell the truth I was very fed up myself, but had to let on that I wasn't. I mean, I couldn't let them see that they'd been right about my not being able to get a job if I arsed about at school, or that I'd be too dumb to hold one down if I ever did land one. Also I was getting worried that I might have to spend the rest of my life on the dole queue, taking hand-outs, and having to say, 'Oh, thank you, kind sir,' for a few quid. It's part of my daft character that I hate having to thank anyone for anything. I like people thanking me for favours I do them, but not the other way round. Same as I like giving presents but dread receiving them.

Then some of my mates started getting into trouble with the law, doing really stupid things just because they'd nothing else to do. Nothing very serious to begin with – a bit of shoplifting, pointless vandalism, things like that. After a bit, though, it got more serious: house-breaking, car theft, and even robbery with threats. I wasn't so thick I couldn't see I'd soon end up doing that sort of mindless shit if I didn't watch out, and when one bloke I knew got sent down for three years it really put the wind up me. But what the hell was I going to do?

One evening Mam and me were alone in the house. Mam said, 'Phil, your Dad and me are getting really fed up about you, you know.'

'I'm okay, Mam.'

'You're not okay. Why don't you get yourself a steady job and settle down like everyone else?'

'I'm trying.'

'No you're not.'

'Yes I am.'

'You're not. You're just spending your days messing about with those friends of yours in Lancaster. I've heard all about it. People have seen you, you know. You're just going to end up in dead trouble before you're much older, and that'll be that.'

'Not me, Mam.'

'Yes, you.'

That's all we said, but for some reason it kept playing

on my mind, probably because I knew Mam was right again, and me wrong, as usual. Right, I said to myself, I'll bloody show them. Tomorrow I'll get a job no matter what it is, I decided. Mind you, I was nice and snug in my bed at the time, and bed's a great place to be positive and optimistic, isn't it? You can do anything you want with the blankets pulled over your head.

TWO

'You haven't!' Mam exclaimed when I told her, sounding, it struck me, amazed and relieved.

'I have,' I said.

'Did you hear that, Alan? Our Phil's joined the Army.'

'Good,' was all Dad had to say. He never says much when the television is on, and the television is on morning noon and night, even if no one is watching it.

All of which was a bit of an anticlimax after me keeping it all bottled up inside, and wondering for months if I'd been really out of my mind to sign on in the first place. I was glad nobody asked me why I'd joined up, because I had no idea, only that it seemed like a good idea at the time. I'd gone to Lancaster for no particular reason, probably just to get away from home for a few hours. I was getting pretty sick of Dad always asking me when I was going to get a job, and Mam looking at me accusingly but not saying anything – not saying anything to me, that is, but moaning to Dad in the evenings when they thought I wasn't listening, both of them agreeing that I could never do anything right, that I was going to end up in trouble if I didn't watch out, and why couldn't I show some ambition? Anyway, there I was, suddenly, outside the recruitment office in Lancaster, although how I actually got there is anyone's guess since it's tucked up in a narrow back alley behind a hotel, like they were really ashamed of it or something.

'Come in!'

And then I was in the recruitment officer's room. It stank, I remember, of stale cigarette smoke. There were lots of glossy posters on the walls, all with different coloured edging, explaining the advantages of an army career to morons like me. There was a long metal table and two chairs. In one of the chairs was a staff sergeant, small, I thought for a staff sergeant, but you could have peeled potatoes with the crease in his trousers and shaved yourself in the shine of his boots.

While I was looking at him, he was staring at me, of course, and I could tell he wasn't thrilled by what he saw. Well, maybe my hair *was* a bit long, and perhaps I should have shaved, and I suppose torn jeans and a T-shirt with Pink Floyd written across it isn't everyone's cup of tea. He had an odd sort of glint in his eye and I had a bet with myself that he was stripping me down and dressing me up again in uniform and enjoying the torture he'd put me through in between.

'Well, sonny, what can we do for you?' he asked finally.

I wanted to tell him I wasn't his goddamn sonny. To tell the truth I wanted to get out of the place as fast as I could. But I shrugged, trying to be casual, and said, 'I just wanted to know what the crack is for me to get into the Army.'

He didn't think much of that. His eyes narrowed and the smile he had forced on to his lips collapsed like it had been switched off at the mains.

'It's no crack, sonny,' he said, and there was a bit of menace in his voice. Then he beamed again, and started being really witty. 'We'll have to smarten you up, laddy,' he said, somehow making me feel I should be truly grateful for that. 'Your hair, now, you won't be needing those pretty tresses to help your mates over the obstacle course, will you?'

I didn't laugh because I didn't think that was very funny. I mean, I think it's just ignorant to mock people because of their appearance. What the hell difference does it make what someone looks like if they're nice themselves, nice inside?

It kind of threw him when I kept a straight face. I could just imagine other recruits bursting their guts laughing at his stupid dig just to keep him happy. He switched tack and got down to being serious, maybe thinking that if he wasn't careful I might be one fish he wouldn't hook. I wondered then if he got a commission for every sucker he conned; I wondered, too, what they might pay him since that would give me an idea of what I was worth to them.

'This,' he said, handing me a form, 'you take to your doctor right away. You have one, I suppose?'

'Yeah.'

'Who is he?'

'Doctor Higton.'

'In?'

'Here. Lancaster.'

That pleased him. 'Good, good. You can nip round there now, can't you, and have the examination? Then back here. Right?'

'Right,' I said, like a dummy.

The medical was a laugh. Doctor Higton had the time of his life. He poked and prodded and pinched and squeezed like I was a joint of beef or something. He tested my eyes for vision, naturally, and for colour-blindness too. Then he told me to undress. He weighed me and checked my lungs. He tapped my knees and elbows with a little mallet for reflexes. I was tempted to bring my foot up really quick and clobber him, but he was only doing his job. Next thing he was on the floor looking at my feet. You can't have flat feet in the Army, you know. Your mind can be as flat as you like, but not your feet.

The last thing he did was test my ears. He went off across the room and started whispering at me. I could hear him all right, but I really wanted to joke a bit. When he said, 'Can you hear me?' I wanted to say, 'Ten to eleven, I think,' but decided I'd better not. Maybe that would be pushing things too far. He didn't seem like a man with much sense of humour. I suppose having to watch people die all your life would knock it out of you. 'That was quick,' the recruitment officer said when I came back.

'Yeah. I'm a really fast worker.'

He ignored that, and read the doctor's report, muttering away and nodding to himself as if he really understood it. It took him a while as he had to mouth every word to make it sink in. Then he started flicking through some papers on his desk. 'Right,' he said finally. 'I want you back here, let me see, next Thursday — that's six days' time — for the first of your acceptance exams.'

'Exams?' That shook me.

'Yes, laddy. Exams. We don't take just anyone in the Army, you know.'

'Oh.'

'You'll be one of the élite. People will look up to you when you're in uniform.'

'Oh sure.'

I suppose he meant that nobody looked up to you if you're *not* in uniform, which doesn't hold out much hope for anyone else, does it? Mind you, if you knew the questions they asked in the selection and entrance tests you'd probably think your four-year-old kid was eligible for the army. I mean, to fail you'd really have to be a right plonker and thick as two planks. In fact, it would probably be harder to fail than to pass, but then they don't exactly encourage intelligence in the ranks. Leads to lack of moral, you see. It would never do for the mere privates to realise how dumb some of the officers are.

So, a week later I turned up as scruffy as ever and did my first test. Easy stuff, a list of simple logical problems like they give chimpanzees to do, using shapes and colours. There were a few maths problems to solve as well, but they were just as childish. I was finished in half an hour, which shook the old recruitment officer. 'Clever little dick, eh?' he said.

'You said it.'

He was surprised, too, at the results. He told me a bit grudgingly that I'd scored well and could now qualify for selection. Which meant more tests.

'You won't find those so easy,' he told me.

'Want to bet?'

He set the selection date for about a month later. He then handed me the traditional one day's pay, and told me I was to report to the selection centre in Sutton Coldfield on the date prescribed. He then gave me rail travel tickets. 'Good luck,' he said. 'You'll bloody need it with your attitude.'

'I'll get by,' I told him.

'Want to bet,' was his answer, and we both had a bit of a laugh at that.

He was right when he said the second lot of tests would be harder. They were a bit, but not much. They didn't tell me right away how I'd done, but I knew I'd done okay, and I was quite cheerful when I set off for home again to wait.

Six months later I got this letter telling me that someone had the pleasure of informing me that I'd been accepted, and that's when I broke the news at home that I'd joined up.

'And the Guards too,' Mam said to Dad.

'Good,' Dad said, wincing in case he missed some of that esoteric dialogue going on between Dempsey and Makepeace.

'The Scots Guards,' Mam persisted, like I'd been canonised.

'Good,' said Dad.

'I'm really proud of you, Phil,' Mam told me.

If it was good enough for my Dad it was good enough for me. 'Good,' I said, and left it at that.

THREE

There's a photograph of me hanging in my Mam's sitting room, and every time I look at it now it's like looking at someone else. It was taken shortly after I enlisted and I'm in my uniform of the Scots Guards in front of an armoured car, the rim of my cap jammed level with my nose. I tell you this because if you ever want to see the face of a young fascist you really should take a look at it. And I'm not blaming the Army either. I was like that before I joined up. And racist, too, probably because I kept hearing people say dumb things like 'If it wasn't for those niggers and Pakis there'd be plenty of work for our lads', and, 'If they'd listened to Enoch Powell the country wouldn't be in the mess it is.' Mind you, the blacks I came across in the Army were pretty racist too, so I suppose it works both ways.

That September I reported like a good boy to the Guards Depot at Purbright. It was pouring with rain and, honestly, the place looked like a real concentration camp. The barracks were a mass of office departments and what they call spider-blocks – avenues of old-fashioned asbestos buildings which turned out to be our dormitories. And the noise was immense. Everyone was on the move. Squads of new recruits doing drill practice, or being double-marched to ranges armed with live weapons, or coming in from assault courses all muddy and sweating, looking a bit dazed and wondering what the hell they'd let themselves in for. And you know the way sergeants are depicted in films, bull-necked and bellowing? Well, the ones I saw that first day all seemed to be just like that, roaring their heads off and keeping everyone else on the move.

Anyway, me and the other recruits who had travelled down together were shown our spider, and before we could recover from the shock we were being briefed on fire drills and told how we were expected to keep the billets clean. Then we were kitted out with piles of khaki clothing and gas masks, helmets, and boots, and none of us could manage to fit all this crap into our kitbags.

They move fast in the Army. I think the idea behind it is that if you don't have time to think you won't start realising what a pillock you've been to get involved with the military. Keep the sodding buggers on the go, was the motto, and they certainly did that. Within what – ten weeks? About that – I'd been drilled and marched stupid, done cross-country runs with my kitbag filled with sand, and been forced to get over the fear of heights – something I'd never been afraid of anyway. Also I'd learned how to kill people efficiently with high-velocity rifles, sub-machine-guns, anti-tank rocket projectors, heavy machine guns, and was soon pretty nifty with the old hand grenades.

The big deal was, of course, that this was the *Scots* Guards, not your poxy Irish Guards or Grenadiers. So when we weren't up to our necks in mud or weapons, we were getting lectures on the past glories of our regiment, and supposedly being impressed by the battle honours gained at the Somme and El Alamein. The lecturer kept stressing the number of Guards who'd been killed and it struck me then that to be dead was much better than coming back alive, although I didn't think too much about it.

And then there was the bagpipe and bugle sessions. These, would you believe, took place in the shower room since the acoustics there were better. We had to stand there and listen to that godawful noise as the piper wheezed away, and then we'd have to identify the tune. They all sounded the same to me. I mean, one cat screeching sounds just like any other cat screeching, doesn't it?

So now I was a soldier and ready to be a credit to Queen and country. We were, as they put it, introduced to our units. I was sent to Chelsea and had my ceremonial uniform tailored and fitted. When it was finished and I looked at myself in the mirror I was the proudest thing on two feet. I looked really terrific, even if I say so myself. Just to get that uniform made everything worthwhile. I was great. The Army was great. The whole bloody world was great. You can imagine what I felt like when I was on duty at Buckingham Palace. Me. Phil Williams. Guarding the Queen! It was two hours' duty, four hours' rest for twenty-four hours, and I couldn't wait for the rest periods to end. Of course, being soldiers, we spent the rest periods polishing boots and brass and moaning our heads off about what a waste of time it was, although none of us really meant it. I made sure all my kit gleamed because I had the daft feeling that every time any of the royals went past they looked directly at me. Crazy, I know, but that's how it was.

Chelsea was pretty okay, you know. They have their own shops there, a bar, swimming pool, gymnasium. Basically all we did was to keep fit. They made us do lots of long-distance running which I hated since I couldn't see the point, really, of running somewhere just to run back again. We played soccer, and did some orienteering which was interesting. Map reading too, which would have been useful to me later if I'd had a map, which I hadn't.

I was with my unit about three months, and we were getting ready for the Trooping of the Colour, and what happened? I broke my leg, that's what happened. Quite badly as it turned out. So instead of strutting about on parade before all the world I was in Woolwich Hospital. Jesus, I was furious. I'd really been looking forward to that ceremony and, like everyone else, was all geared up and ready to go. I watched it on the telly, and I'll confess that I had a bit of a cry to myself, but I cheered myself up by trying to spot the mistakes that were made – not by the Scots Guards, of course. We never made mistakes.

I was a patient in Woolwich for nearly eight months, so you can see it was a pretty severe smash my leg had taken, although much of that time was spent at home on leave, going to Woolwich from time to time for therapy.

I had to move about on crutches, and the neighbours had a great time taking the piss out of me, saying, trust me to be wounded without there ever being a war. Mind you, nobody was thinking about war then. 'Oh, trust our Phil. If there's an accident waiting to happen, he'll find it.'

When my leg was declared fit I went back to Chelsea. I was glad to be back. I felt sort of secure and at home. I only had time to do just one public duty before the Falklands were invaded. Then the Scots Guards were deployed as part of the task force, and preparations began.

FOUR

I thought it was weird sending us to Wales for our last bit of training. But they knew what they were doing, all right. The part of Wales we went to was every bit as desolate and windswept as the Falklands were to be. We all agreed that we now knew why all the Welsh were so mad: you'd need to be out of your mind to want to live there voluntarily. It took us five hours to get there by truck convoy, but it passed okay for some of us – those of us that had a bit of hash that is.

There were the usual dormitories at the camp but we weren't allowed to use them. We were issued with tents and told to erect them on the sports field. This, they said, was the base camp for operations. For the first while we just did extra weapon training and learned the art of digging trenches, and, believe me, there is an art to it. The food was cooked in a field kitchen and was really shitty. Most of us went hungry rather than eat it. In the evenings we'd just sit around waiting for something interesting to happen. Myself and a few mates would get nicely doped and listen to the others ranting on about how they'd give their right arms for a pint, or a woman, but always a pint first. That's all they ever talked about, like as if they were afraid they'd be called queer if they brought up any halfway intelligent subject.

Then the Army started taking us out to firing ranges, moving us there in either trucks or helicopters. We made mock attacks on various positions, the Gurkhas acting as the enemy. One halfwit asked me, 'Why the Gurkhas, Phil? Is that what the Argies look like?'

'Yeah,' I said. 'Only they're bigger. And they've no hair. And the ones from the north have only one eye in the centre of their forehead.'

It'll give you some idea what I was dealing with when I tell you he believed me. And he didn't have the chance to find out I was having him on since he was killed before he ever set eyes on one.

The main exercise came after a couple of weeks – to get us prepared for the real thing, we were told. It was a tactical attack using the whole brigade plus support from Harriers and tanks. There were random targets and we had to run at these screaming our heads off and firing like crazy. I never found out why they wanted us to scream but I suppose some dim-witted officer had been watching too many Green Beret movies. The air strike was impressive though: Harriers swooping in down the valley in front of us, dropping bombs. They recorded this for TV propaganda.

One night they gave us 'long fire-power' demonstrations. We were stood in rows of trenches while machine guns and mortars were fired into a sandbank behind us. It certainly was pretty effective; the way the live rounds lit up in long, tracing, laser-like movements was lovely.

And then, without knowing it, we were ready to go to war. We were given four days' leave and told the QE2 was being refitted as a troop carrier. We were also told to keep our mouths shut, but you could see half the lads were dying to get home and impress their girlfriends by telling them they were off to save the Falklands. Me, I didn't really believe I was going. Even when I had to centralise my equipment and make sure it all worked properly, and was issued with special Arctic clothing, and had a dog-tag hung about my neck, I couldn't really see myself going to war. Phil Williams didn't get involved in that sort of thing, did he? He was in the army to guard the Palace, and to parade, and to be told how smart he looked and how proud his Mam was.

One laugh we did get was when we were briefed on basic Spanish. For ages we called each other *Señor*, which was the only word we picked up, and a lot of good that was going to prove.

Anyway, we were given some of our wages and, ready or not to rally before the flag, I left Euston for Lancaster.

FIVE

It's funny. When you get out of uniform and away from the Army, even for a few days, you think, God, that's great. But it doesn't take you long to change your mind and think it's not so great after all. Even though you don't think all that much of your mates, you miss them suddenly. And you miss the Army. I'm not saying that we got brainwashed or anything like that, but it's a bit like being in prison, I suppose. You never have to make up your own mind about anything; they do that for you. And they provide everything: clothes, bedding, food. So, in a way, your mind stops working, and that's pretty dangerous when you come to think of it.

Maybe that's why I was feeling a bit depressed when I arrived in Lancaster. I visited my parents, but only stayed there a day. Already I'd changed quite a bit, maybe grown up, and I couldn't stand Mam wanting to know everything and treating me like a child again.

I had this girlfriend at the time, Alison. Nothing serious, just a girlfriend like everyone else. I spent the other three days with her. We'd drive out into the country, North Yorkshire mostly. I remember we drank a lot, and had sex a lot outdoors, which was nice, but to me it was like I was just filling in time. Nothing romantic. She kept asking me if I loved her, and I'd say, sure I do, just to keep her quiet since I didn't feel like having unnecessary stupid rows about who loved who.

Then leave was over and it was time for me to go. I don't to this day know why, but I couldn't bring myself to say goodbye to Mam. I just set out for the station with Alison, leaving Mam thinking I'd be back in ten minutes. I didn't mean to be cruel or anything like that. One thing I'm not is cruel.

It looked like all hell had broken loose in Chelsea Barracks. Everyone was shouting and trucks were being loaded and machinery prepared. I was glad to be back, even though the weather was hot, and I could see my mates were too, but none of us said so, of course. We moaned and groaned and agreed it was fucking awful to be back.

We had just half the night left, and most of the lads went up the West End to get drunk. I didn't. I went to Battersea Park. To tell the truth I'd picked up some good pot in Lancaster and wanted to have a decent smoke and a bit of a think by myself. I remember my Mam saying to an aunt of mine, 'The trouble with our Phil is he thinks too much.' But I don't think *too* much or, at least, I didn't then. But it's really nice to get away by yourself and let different thoughts drift in and out of your head, and take your time about sorting out any problems you have. That's what I did in Battersea, just sort of daydreamed. And, come to think of it, it was the last time I was able to be on my own like this.

The transport left for Southampton at 4.30 a.m. You'd have thought we were travelling by hearse, it was that quiet; everyone exhausted or sobering up, or maybe, for the first time, getting jittery and nervous, and not daring to say anything in case they gave themselves away.

For some reason I thought it would be cooler at Southampton, but it wasn't. It was hotter than in Chelsea, a steamy, sticky kind of hot. We were all lined up and then marched up the gangway. I'd never been on a ship before, unless you count the ferry to the Isle of Man. Neither had any of the other lads and they were all horsing around like kids on an outing, shouting out when they found the shops or the showers or the toilets. There were a lot of arguments, too. We were four to each double cabin, and what with all our gear and weapons there wasn't much room. With everyone sweating the smell started to get pretty bad; not as bad as at night when we took off our boots, but bad enough.

By noon a crowd had assembled on the dock. They held up banners with names on them – Good Luck Jimmy – that sort of crap. A couple of girls took their clothes off and started vamping up and down on top of those big ferry containers. If they heard what we said about them they'd have got dressed again pretty damn quick.

When the ship started to pull out the shore was a

mass of red, white and blue, and everyone was cheering and calling out, and I don't mind admitting I felt really choked and had tears in my eyes.

We had a good time on the voyage. Sure, we had to do physical exercise and some target practice, but most of the time we swam in the pools or played five-a-side soccer. We had a few abandon-ship exercises too, and lectures about the Falkland Islands landscape, but we'd knock off about 4.30 p.m. and then watch movies or drink ourselves stupid on duty-free beer. That meant that some of the yobos were getting sick all over the place, but as long as they didn't do it in my cabin I wasn't about to complain.

We anchored in the Bay of South Georgia. Then it was all quick, quick, quick again, collecting all the equipment and assembling for a ferry to take us to another expensive conversion, the SS *Canberra*. If it had been cramped on the *QE2* we were like sardines on the *Canberra*. There wasn't room to do anything active, so all we did was read and sleep. Still there was a cabaret in the large lounge and the bright boys had to join in to show how witty they were, telling jokes and singing or playing the piano or whatever turn they could.

All the while we were sailing closer to the Falklands, and sometimes we were called on to do anti-aircraft duty. I found this exciting, like something was happening at last, although the weather was atrocious and my stomach kept heaving. Often there were escorts of battle-ships watching over us. The only thing that scared me at that time was the thought of having to abandon ship and swim for it, since I'm not the greatest swimmer in the world and I couldn't see my doggie paddle getting far in that rough sea.

Finally we hove to – that's navy talk for stopping. As the landing craft were assembling alongside the liner we were issued with extra ammo. I was given two bloody great shells to carry. I had the idea of just dropping the damn things overboard, since together with my own rifle and backpack I couldn't see myself getting very far.

Hanging around, waiting for my turn to board the landing craft, I got my first glimpse of the Falklands and wondered why the hell anyone would want to own it in the first place. Barren and treeless and grey, with a climate that on good days was foggy but mostly just rained and rained or, for a laugh, there were hailstones.

We walked off the jetty and inland, uphill of course. Every damn step you took on that place seemed to be uphill. Endlessly going up and never coming down. That's the way it felt, anyway. There were soldiers everywhere, either digging in or sitting there with big machine guns, staring at the sky. There'd been dozens of landings like ours and the ground was well chewed up, making my load seem twice as heavy.

After about a two-hour slog the company was placed in the usual all-round defence. It was time to dig in. That caused language that would have made the Mummies at home turn white. All that happened when you dug was that the water poured in, so the deeper you dug the more

water you had to cope with. I noticed the liner start
sailing away and wished to hell I was back on it. If this
was war they could keep it.

We stayed there for about a week, soaking wet, miserable, unable to credit that it could keep on raining and
snowing the way it did. You wouldn't really be able to
understand what it was like unless you've had your home
flooded, and those trenches were our home. As it rained,
the water came down from the mountains in torrents
into the trenches, into our boots, into our sleeping bags.
Somebody said, 'You need fucking webbed feet to live
in a place like this.' He was right.

I've never found out really what we were supposed to
be doing there. Maybe some officer made a cock-up
which couldn't be admitted. The next thing we knew we
were being herded back to the landing craft and sent out
to HMS *Antelope*. The craft sailed right into the dry
dock in the hull of the *Antelope*, and you could see
everyone cheering up a bit as we realised how warm and
dry it was. The hull was filled with Land Rovers and big
guns: they had to be kept warm and dry, whatever
happened to us.

We only stayed on board until dark, just long enough
for us to start enjoying it. Then it was back to the landing
craft again. Actually I never heard the order to board as
I was having a nice little kip under a jeep. It didn't take
them long to find me though, and I got a right bollocking,
being told, 'We're at war now, soldier,' as if I hadn't
realised that.

I don't know how long we were on the craft but it

seemed like a bloody lifetime. There was no cover at all from the sea that lashed over the side, and we were all soaked again in seconds. We just huddled on the floor of the craft. Not speaking. Unable to smoke. Fed up.

We landed on a shingle beach. For a couple of hours we just sat there, freezing. Naturally it was pissing down. Then someone kindly told us where we were. It was a place I'd never heard of, not that anyone else had. It was called Bluff Cove.

You should have heard the groans and curses when the order came for us to march to the Bluff Cove Settlement. We could barely move. All our joints had frozen, I think. But off we went through the muck. It took about an hour to get there, and by the time we did everyone was steaming, thick steam like we were on fire. The Settlement was on the shore: three houses and farms, gun trenches around the houses. The owner of the slaughterhouse said we could sleep in there. Jesus, it stank and there were bits of sheep scattered all over the place, but it was dry. So I hung my clothes on one of the hooks they used for hanging up the carcasses and crawled into my sleeping bag. I was that tired I didn't wake up once during the night.

A major shouted, 'No shitting on the beach. You're not bloody Paras.'

What he didn't know was that there were a few Paras in the slaughterhouse and one of them called back, 'How can you tell it's not Scots shit, you ignorant cunt?' I thought the major would burst a blood vessel.

Later that morning we were ferried across the inlet of Bluff Cove, and from there we marched a couple of miles to a spot above the cove. We were told to dig in and wait again. I got to share a rather well-built shelter with Sergeant Gribble and a corporal whose name I can't remember. They were okay, those two NCOs. We had a few laughs as we furnished the shelter with moss and heather. 'Like fucking hens,' the sergeant said, and made it nice and comfy. We took turns on watch in a machine-gun trench.

There were flames in the distance. Always in the distance, I was thinking. Then we were shelled for the first time. It was just before dark, and the shells were too damn close and frightened the life out of me. The noise they made was terrific. But it's true that you get used to anything, and pretty soon we got used to the shelling, treating it more or less like we treated the rain – a bloody nuisance.

Looking down over Bluff Cove I could see the *Sir Galahad* and the *Sir Tristram*. Like two big white buildings, they were.

The choppers were taking stores ashore. A couple of Argie fighters came out of nowhere and bombed both ships. I opened fire on the planes. One was shot down but I don't think I hit it.

The fires burned on the ships for about three days. After that they were towed to deeper water and sunk. I remember crying. I thought there was something evil about a system that took the stores off first and left the men on board to be killed. I said so to the corporal but he just shrugged, like he was telling me not to expect any better.

Most of us got diarrhoea. We were all filthy. We knew that. We could smell each other a mile away, which probably made Sergeant Morcom's order for us to wash seem all the more stupid. Not that anyone paid much attention to him. Then he started screaming that we were all to shave, like he was Alec Guinness on the River Kwai. Sergeant Gribble got really pissed off at that and told him to fuck off. It was good fun for us to see the two sergeants having a go at each other. Best laugh we'd had in ages.

Told to assemble again. Being flown to a place called Tumbledown. Flight cancelled due to bad weather. Wait two more days. Assemble again. Ten minutes flight. Dropped in a valley with mountains all round it. Assemble again. Dig in again. Wait again.

SIX

I don't know if everyone or even anyone else felt the same, but for me the thing they call war only started at Tumbledown. Don't ask me why since I can't give a reason. It wasn't that much different but there seemed to be something different about the fighting, as if up until then we'd been practising, and now this was the real thing. As we were digging in shells were landing all round us and our artillery was firing back, the shells whizzing over our heads. I could feel the ground shudder under my feet and thought I could sense the wind of the shells on my face, which was stupid. But maybe that was it: for the first time I could *feel* the danger. And there were a few injuries from the explosions, which made one think. That could have been me, you thought, but the thought had a bit of a swagger in it, like you were far too clever for it *really* to happen to you.

As the injured were carried in on stretchers nobody looked at them. I didn't either. I suppose we were all scared we might see images of ourselves lying there all maimed and bloody. Not that I was afraid of dying.

When you're my age you don't even think that it's possible, not even when people are shooting at you. But I didn't want to be injured. That was the thing all of us dreaded, I think. Injury was far worse than death in our minds. At that time anyway.

Crazy.

The shells were still blasting away when Sergeant Gribble started handing out mail like a macabre Postman Pat.

There was one for me. From Mam. I hate writing letters so I know it must have been hard for her to find something to say but – well – you want to know what she wrote? She works in an old folks' home and she spent the whole letter telling me about this resident with no relatives who'd died and how the entire staff of the home had turned out to make up a crowd. Cheerful stuff! I mean, I felt sad for the old person dying all alone but I didn't particularly want to hear about it, not when I might be following her myself at any moment. Not that I'd be alone, I'd have the whole battalion around me. But that's not the same. When you're dying you need someone really precious beside you: you need someone like that more when you're dying than while you're alive.

Word came that we were moving out. We were to centralise all our equipment and leave everything behind except ammo, weapons, water, and one day's food ration. That was a laugh. We didn't have any food. Hadn't had any for a day or two.

We were lined up in formations for our advance on Tumbledown. Everyone cocked their rifles. Funny sound, all that clicking. It reminded me of something but I couldn't remember what. Then off we went, marching into the cold night. Hey, maybe we were yomping! I never thought of that.

Whatever we were doing, we did it for about three hours. Like I said, all uphill. The shell fire was really heavy now, so we were ordered to take cover. We'd started sweating during the ascent and now that we stopped we started to freeze. If you've never had the sweat freeze on you, you're lucky. It's the coldest thing you can imagine. Two of the lads keeled over with exposure. I wasn't feeling that great myself. Snipers were now taking pot shots at us which didn't help. I swear you could hear their bullets zinging off the rocks. I thought that happened only in Westerns.

One shell landed particularly close and I could feel the blast of the explosion hitting me. It didn't blow me over like I'd expected. It was like as if it had got inside me and blown outwards. Really weird. Funny thing was I found it exciting.

A major came to our platoon. He wanted volunteers. Four volunteers. He didn't say what for. Genius here had his hand up like a shot. As soon as I had it up I wanted to take it down again. The lads were looking at me hard. Some like I was out of my mind. Some like I was being really brave. For some reason that irked me. I didn't want them to think I was trying to be some sort of hero. Shit. I promised to tell the truth. I *did* want them to think I was brave. But that's not the true reason I volunteered. I was so cold and so bored and so miserable I'd have done anything to get moving, and volunteering was the only option open. Mind you, if I'd known that my heroics were to change my whole bloody life I don't know that I'd have been so damn quick off the mark.

'Make yourselves as light as possible,' the major said.

I discarded everything but my rifle, some ammo, a water bottle, some field dressing.

'You'll need to be nifty dodging the snipers,' the major explained.

We gawped at him.

He pointed up Tumbledown. 'Just look for casualties,' he said, as if he meant 'just look for mushrooms.' Or daisies.

It started snowing. A real blizzard with a bitter wind whipping it up in swirls. It was difficult to get a footing since it was all rocky, and the rocks were like glass. Maybe it would have been okay if we could just have concentrated on the climbing, but we had to duck and dive all the time since the Argies were having the time of their lives using us as target practice. And all the time it was running through my mind that if I *did* slip I could easily break my leg again, and maybe there'd be no one daft enough to come out and haul me in.

We got five casualties back. Each time we got one on the stretcher there'd be another one falling beside us, injured or dead. We were knackered. 'Keep going men,' the major said, and off we went again.

Later someone said to me that it must have been awful having to carry my mates down on stretchers seeing them injured. It wasn't. There was something really satisfying about it. And anyway, what's the point in anything if you can't help somebody who needs help?

One of the casualties was a chap I knew quite well, Jim Mitchell. I said to him, trying to cheer him up, 'Typical of you, Mitchell, trying to hitch an easy lift back, you lazy sod.'

He tried to smile but blood came out of his mouth. That was awful all right.

My turn to hand over the stretcher and carry the kit. It was very heavy and I was having an awful struggle to keep up. I hadn't a free hand to keep the snow out of my eyes. My legs were giving way with fatigue, and I kept sliding back further than I advanced.

I don't know why but for a second everything seemed to get terribly quiet. Then the shell landed close to me with a terrific explosion. I remember thinking, 'God, this is a hell of a way to die,' because someone had said that in some book I'd read. Then everything went black.

SEVEN

It's going to be hard for me to tell you what happened
next since I don't really know myself. I want to say that
everything was like a dream but that sounds stupid.
Anyway, it wasn't quite like a dream. It was very real
but hazy, like I was swimming in and out of conscious-
ness. The funny thing is I must have known it would be
important for me to try and recall things, because that's
when I started writing my observations down. Some of
them don't make sense to me, so God alone knows what
you'll make of them. And the language I used was pretty
rough. It might shock you. It shocked me I admit, but
only because I'd never realised I was that crude. Of
course I used to swear like the rest of the lads but I can't
understand why I bothered to write down the swear
words. I asked a doctor about it later and he told me I'd
used it as a defence. I still haven't worked out what he
meant by that. Anyway, if you'll just bear with me I'll
try and work my way through it all again.

You know how it is when you've been very tired and
had a very deep sleep and just woken up there's a few

seconds when you're not asleep but not quite awake either. Well, that's how I felt when I came round. I couldn't move and I thought, Oh Christ, I've been paralysed. I really wanted to cry but didn't dare since I got this idea that if I did my tears would freeze and I'd be blinded into the bargain. I just lay there and closed my eyes and let myself fall away again.

Must have been dreaming. Thought I was paralysed. But I'm walking okay. Can feel my legs but not my feet. Maybe they've dropped off. Stupid asshole. Course they haven't dropped off.

Must climb. Make for the high ground. Look about and see what there is to see. Why did the fuckers go off and leave me? So hungry. Must eat. Get to the high ground first though ... Take to the high ground, me hearties, said John Wayne.

Biscuits taste good. Dry but good. So much for the high ground – can't see a fucking thing. Only snow falling. Thick snow like a solid sheet. Nothing like a hot bath, then into bed with clean white sheets, is there?

Snow stopped. No rain. No wind. Very still. Nothing but mountain peaks and valleys. In the distance across the peat moors there's the shoreline. Jesus, I'm tired. Kip a bit before deciding what to do. Good idea.

Wonder if anyone's looking for me. If anyone cares.

I don't know how long I slept. I didn't have a clue how long it was since the explosion had happened. I woke up feeling quite good mentally, although it took me ages to get any sort of feeling back into my body. Especially my damn legs and feet. There didn't seem to be enough warm blood in me to reach them.

It was a bright enough day for once, bright by Falklands standards that is. We'd call it murky. But it wasn't snowing or raining. I climbed further along the ridge, pleased that I could at least see where I was putting my feet. I stopped and gazed around. Jesus, it was a desolate bloody place, all grey and drab and unpretty, the sort of place you'd think people would be glad to give away rather than try and hang on to. It struck me as really pathetic that two big countries were fighting each other over this miserable shit-hole. Of course the ones who were making the decisions weren't doing the actual fighting, and I'll bet that none of their sons were getting killed either. Then I started to laugh out loud, not proper laughter, mean stuff, because I remembered how when Mark Thatcher got himself lost in the desert nearly every bloody helicopter in Europe was out looking for him, and there was me, poor little Phil Williams, lost in the bog and they wouldn't send up one lousy chopper to take a look.

After a bit more walking I spotted, away in the distance, what looked like a white farm unit. I decided I'd go there for help.

To get to the farmhouse I had to come down off the ridge, and in so doing lose sight of the farm buildings. I wasn't sure I was going in the right direction; I just hoped to hell I was. At the same time I was feeling quite jittery since Christ alone knows what might be waiting for me if I did reach it.

Came across a defence position. Trenches all round. Craters everywhere. Found an Argie helmet and thought it would make a good souvenir. Wondered what the bloke's name had been. Nearly shit myself when I picked it up and found half a head still inside, stuck there. Puked my guts out and flung the helmet as far as I could manage. Heard it ping off the rocks and rattle away, scattering the Argie's brains everywhere. Odd no sign of his body. Sad that they took that and left half his head behind, not that he'd need it. They don't half shit a lot, these Argies. Shit all over the place. Not in little piles like you'd expect. Little trails, like they were running and shitting at the same time. Maybe the poor sods were.

Getting really weak and tired. Can't see the bloody croft. Must have gone wrong somewhere. Nothing but bog. Going in circles, maybe. Round and round. Fuck it. Skin between my toes cracking open, stinging like hell from the sweat. I keep thinking I can smell roast pork and veg. Christ, that would be nice. A bit of crackling to chew on. I remember somewhere seeing a woman with a pretty little baby on her knee. She was playing 'This Little Piggie Went to Market'. Bouncing him up and down, making him laugh and giggle. Can't help thinking that I'd eat his pink little toes now if I had the chance.

Suddenly I saw the farm only about half a mile away, and I made my way towards it. I don't think I blinked once during that walk in case it would disappear like a mirage.

There was a small gate leading into the croft. I was about to open it when something made me look down. Lucky I did. There was this antipersonnel mine sitting there by the gatepost just waiting for me. That woke me up.

I climbed the gate and very carefully and silently made my way to one of the outbuildings. I squatted there for a while, looking about. I could hear water running and realised how dry my mouth was. I decided to explore. Cautiously. And I found a spring. I drank the water and splashed some on my face. It tasted really good but, Christ, it was cold on my skin. Then, of course, it struck me that the bastards might have poisoned the water. Fuck it, I thought. Too late to worry now. I'm probably going to freeze to death anyway.

It took a while for it to dawn on me how quiet everything was. The farmhouse was deserted. There wasn't much sign of fighting, but a couple of windows had been blown in and the door was wide open. I got down on all fours and crept inside.

It was tiny. There was just the kitchen, two bedrooms, a bathroom and a loft. I started poking about.

In one of the bedrooms there was a dead soldier.

There was quite a stink off him so he must have been there for some time. He was lying face down and looked comfortable enough.

The other bedroom was empty, but the kitchen floor was littered with broken radios and maps and backpacks. There was a pot of half-prepared food on a peat burner. It had all gone green and mouldy. There were beans in it but they looked like fat white slugs. But there was quite a lot of discarded Army food rations. I gathered some up and really gorged myself. That made me sick. And after I was sick I got hungry again so I ate some more. Best of all there was an iron bed in one corner. I collapsed on to it, and in a second I was snoring my head off.

The next morning, or maybe it was one or two mornings later, I woke up feeling the best I'd felt for a long time. I had some more food but was careful not to overeat this time.

The dead soldier worried me. I thought about burying him decently, but then I thought that if I did that he might never be found and his parents would spend the rest of their lives wondering what had happened to him. I wouldn't want to be responsible for something as awful as that. And, to tell the truth, there was something else: even though he was dead, and even though I never went near him, he was company for me, and during my time around the croft I'd talk to him, and ask his advice, and tell him stupid jokes to cheer him up, and tell him my worries, too, to cheer myself up. Not that I ever went near him. All our conversations were carried on through the closed door.

I planned a strategy. I would use the croft as a base and scout around, trying to get my bearings. Some hope I had. It would take me most of the day to climb the ridge, and when I got there it was always too misty or there was too much snow to see anything. I tried following the coast four days in succession but that didn't get me anywhere either. I could never get far enough. Never really got out of sight of the croft. It was such hard going as the shore curved in and out. I did a hell of a lot more walking than distance.

Saw life today. Animals. Wild ponies, geese, a turkey vulture that looked about as miserable as myself, sitting on a post surrounded by snow, waiting for food. Maybe me. At least that bastard has the prospect of a meal. I don't. Food all gone. Isn't any fucker going to start looking for me?

Tried to make it along the shore again. Came to a low part of the cliff edge and sat down. Had a rest. Only half awake. Can't really seem to be fully awake. Watched the sea crashing in on the rocks. Saw arms and legs and other limbs being washed ashore. Got to wondering if they'd belonged to other people who'd got lost in this fucking place like me. One had stuck up high and started waving at me. Scrambled down to help. Only kelp weed. Shit. Better watch it. Going cracked.

Decided to call my dead friend Pete. Don't know why.
Don't know anyone else called Pete. Maybe that's why.
Hey, Pete, better watch it. I'm going cracked.

And, honestly, a few days later I thought really that I
had gone mad. I know now that it was just some sort of
hallucination, as they call it, but to me, at the time, it
was a sign to me that I'd gone round the bend.

It started snowing very hard during the night. I was
completely cut off in the croft. I wasn't going to risk
going out anyway, not with all those mines and things
littered about. I went up into the loft and lay down, and
fell asleep.

I was woken by soft bangings and scrapings coming
from downstairs. Jesus, that frightened me. Well,
it wasn't so much the noises that frightened me, but
more that I sort of thought I was back with my unit, and
I was going to shout out and tell them where I was
until it dawned on me that it could be Argies down
there waiting to put a bayonet through me. It was the
fact that I might have called for help that frightened
me.

Anyway, after a bit, the noises stopped, so I clambered
down from the loft into the bathroom. I stood in the
doorway facing the kitchen, wondering whether to check
the other rooms or get the hell out of there.

Suddenly there was a shuffling sound coming from
the bedrooms, and voices speaking in Spanish. Fuck me,
I thought, I've only got one bloody grenade – I hope I

don't have to blow myself up. Then everything went quiet again.

I don't honestly know how long I stood there, it seemed like about ten minutes, but it could have been a few seconds or an hour, but the next thing I saw was this dirty-looking bloke in helmet and combat clothing coming into the kitchen followed by a woman and two children. Even now, today, this minute, I can see them. The two kids wore little corduroy dungarees over thick sweaters. They looked scared and very thin, what Mam would call peaky. The man wore an overcoat and wellies. The woman was in jeans and a jumper. They looked scared too. Oh, and a couple of other soldiers followed them into the kitchen, and they had rifles with fixed bayonets.

All the adults seemed to be talking but their lips weren't moving. The soldier leading the group walked up to within two feet of me, looked at me, turned and ordered everyone out of the croft. They trooped past me, and went out into the snow.

I was pretty shattered I can tell you. I went to one of the little windows and looked out. They'd gone. I ran out and peered about for a sign of them. Nothing. There was a hillock to the left and I presumed they'd gone round behind that. It was then I noticed that the only footprints in the snow were my own.

Snow's stopped. Rain today. Two feet of slush outside now. Jesus, it's so fucking cold. Hey, Pete, what d'you think? Yeah, better wait. Conserve energy, as they say.

The slush melted in a day. I started my treks again. All the time I kept trying to find some trace of the people I'd swear I'd seen leaving the croft, and when I'd get back I'd wonder if they'd come back and were waiting for me. The slightest noise and I'd jump. Snow slipping off the roof would sound like footsteps, and sometimes the wind would be like a woman singing.

By now I really was in a bad way. With no food and it being freezing day and night, I was very weak. I started falling asleep for no reason. I'd be walking along and fall asleep. At least I thought I was falling asleep but they told me later I was probably just passing out. No wonder I kept feeling so tired.

One afternoon I was down at the shore again and I'd have bet everything I had that I was in Morecambe. And it was lovely and warm. The sun was blazing away. There was some sort of funfair behind me. I could hear it but didn't look round. The next thing I knew I was lying there with no clothes on like I'd been sunbathing, with about half an inch of snow all over my body. I couldn't feel a thing, numb all over. You can't imagine how comfortable that was, just feeling nothing. I really felt like just staying there, and I don't know what made me change my mind. I'd a terrible job getting dressed again as my uniform was stiff as a board with all the frozen sweat.

Got food today. Goose. Saw a flock of them grazing and tossed a hand grenade into the middle. So hungry I didn't bother to cook it. Just tore it to bits and stuffed the flesh into my mouth and swallowed quick before I could taste it. Used one of the wing feathers to pick my teeth.

The feed made me sleep well. Really *sleep.*

It was funny how every time I went asleep I expected to have nightmares, but I never did. I had dreams, for sure, but nothing nasty or frightening. They were all pretty nice in fact. All about warm rooms and comfy beds and plenty of food and pretty girls.

Ages later someone said to me, 'Christ, it must have been bloody awful sleeping there with a dead body next door.' But it wasn't. Like I said, I never thought of Pete as dead, never thought of him as a person really. More like a toy, like those teddy bears and golliwogs that kids take to bed for comfort. That's what Pete was like, a sort of comforter. I expect what he really did was remind me that I was still alive, and in a way he kept me wanting to stay alive since I didn't care much to end up looking and smelling like him.

Another thing I found out: when you're really tired and exhausted and wondering if you're going to make it, you think of all the crazy little things that you'd forgotten, things that made you laugh like mad when you were very young. Like tying string to someone's knocker and hiding, then pulling the string and watching them come to the door and gape about. I did that quite a bit, especially to one grumpy old bloke who was always giving out to us as kids. Or skipping school and spending the day by the Lune, fishing – poaching really. Really enjoying getting away with it and doing nobody any harm.

I've wondered if maybe I was going through something like the drowning man is supposed to go through, his life flashing through his mind as he sinks for the third time. I suppose I *was* that close to kicking the bucket, only with my short life I didn't have that much to remember.

Of course, being me, there had to be a black side. I had to remember my Dad always telling me that I was useless and could never do anything right. He really *enjoyed* telling me that, I think, because it made *him* feel really clever and useful. And now, stuck there on that bloody island, I'd made a balls up of things again by getting myself lost, and sometimes I'd hear Dad's voice in my sleep, having another go at me, asking me why I couldn't be like so-and-so who was making such a fucking success of his life, and I'd wake up and spend a few minutes telling my Dad where he could shove so-and-so whoever he was.

EIGHT

And maybe it was the feed and the sleep and my feeling a bit better when I woke up that made it dawn on me that the croft was a pretty dangerous place to be. I didn't know it but I'd been there on and off for about a month. Someone was bound to check it out soon, and with my luck it would be the Argies. I made up my mind that I'd leave. I'd just walk out and keep on walking no matter what happened. Just keep walking until I dropped dead or found the platoon.

I felt really sad leaving my little home. It was like being evicted or something. I felt bad about leaving Pete too. I went in to say goodbye to him.

For quite a while I just stood at the door staring at him. Then, I thought, maybe *he's* got a bit of food on him that I could take with me. I went over to him and turned him over. He was lying on his rifle, a complete FN made in Belgium like the Argies use. Yeah, he was an Argie all right, and the bastard was wearing a British combat jacket which he'd probably nicked from a dead Brit. I went a bit berserk at that. I started kicking the

poor sod as if he'd purposely deceived me. And I was
shouting at him, telling him what a dirty fucker he was
for stealing off the dead. It didn't strike me until later
that the poor bastard had only been trying to keep warm
the same way I was. I stripped the jacket off him. It had
the three stripes of a sergeant. It was a hell of a lot better
than my own, so morbidly I gave myself promotion and
put my own jacket over Pete, covering his eyeless face.
Then I started to giggle. I'd thought of the look on
Sergeant Morcom's face if he saw me in a sergeant's
jacket. Then I felt really terrible for kicking old Pete, and
I started to cry. That made me angry with myself. I took
his rifle and some ammo, and left the croft.

That day and the next I followed the coastline, but by
then I could tell I wasn't getting anywhere. I couldn't
understand why I never saw anyone or heard anything
when there was supposed to be this great war going on.

I was searching the outward tide for shellfish, finding
a few and sucking them, and then spitting out the bits
of sand. It seemed to me that the more I ate the hungrier
I got, and the salt water was making me very thirsty,
and my throat was burning. I thought about having a
really great scream, and was on the point of doing just
that when I saw two people on the horizon to my left.
Even at that distance I could tell they were soldiers. They
were walking very slowly, with packs on their backs and
rifles in their hands. I raced off the beach, cursing as my
carefully collected shellfish kept falling out of my helmet.
I got down nicely behind some gorse, and aimed my rifle,

watching them as they moved towards me. As soon as I was sure they weren't British I fired. One of them dropped, and the other took off across the moors. I just lay there trembling and sweating even though I was freezing.

I waited about ten minutes before going to investigate. I was thinking that maybe the dead one had some decent food on him. I was also thinking that I hoped his mate wouldn't get brave and come charging at me with his bayonet.

When I reached the spot where I'd seen the soldier drop there was no trace of him. I wondered if his mate had managed to come and drag him away, but I knew that couldn't have happened. I felt a right idiot having to admit it was another hallucination. I was really angry with myself for losing control. I was twice as angry that there wasn't going to be any food.

I left the coast and started inland. After several miles I came across a couple of sheep that had been blown up. I thought about hacking a piece off one and chewing on that, but they were alive with maggots and I decided starvation was better than eating that crap. From then on I kept passing blown up sheep, so it didn't take much intelligence to know I was walking through a minefield. For a while I was pretty cautious, I can tell you, putting my feet down carefully and waiting then to have my leg blown off. But after a while I started going stupid. I began playing blind-man's-buff, hopping about, and telling the mines they'd missed me. I'd give a little cheer every time I got a few paces intact. I knew I was being daft but I'd got to the stage where I didn't really give a damn. I said so to myself. 'I don't give a *damn*!' I stood still for a while, giggling my stupid head off. 'Frankly, my dear, I don't give a damn,' I said out loud in my lousy best Clark Gable imitation.

Of course I did give a damn, and from then on took bloody good care where I stepped. But even that was done in a light-hearted way, like I was a kid avoiding cowpats. Hunger and fatigue and fright make you really giddy. I can vouch for that.

Another day. Still nothing. NOT A FUCKING THING. *Found four dead Argies huddled together. They didn't seem to be wounded or anything. Just huddled up with their arms about each other in death like they were comforting each other as they died. Lucky bastards. No food on them. Shit, they could have left me something to eat, selfish cunts. Although maybe that's what they died from: starvation. Made a crude little cross out of two sticks and wedged it between the fingers of one of them. Nearly shit myself when I thought he winked at me. Just snow falling off his eyelid. So frigging young, all of them. No more than me. Eighteen. Maybe nineteen. Sergeant Shitface would have gone mad. They hadn't shaved. Don't suppose God's daft enough to care.*

Saw a great flock of birds. Swooping down and settling. Not making any noise. Not their wings or their voices. A bit like crows only with the bills of seagulls, curved at the end and very sharp looking. Bigger than crows too. Went to look at what they found so bloody interesting. Wish now I hadn't. Another dead Argie, half pecked clean. The birds had actually stripped off his combat jacket and the clothes he'd worn under that, and were ripping bits of his flesh and guts out, and swallowing them in gulps, throwing their fucking heads back as they swallowed. Tried chasing them off but they wouldn't budge. The buggers knew they outnumbered me, and I was scared of them. A couple even waddled closer to me to have a look, sizing me up for pudding. Their little eyes were really evil, and they never seemed to blink. Shit, let them have their meal. Anyway, better for the poor sod to have his bones picked clean than to lie there rotting and stinking and looking a mess.

Nearly broke my frigging neck falling into a crater. Didn't even see the damn thing although you could have buried a double-decker bus in it no problem. That's how thick the sleet and rain was. Like a sheet. Couldn't see a thing through it. It had collected in the bottom of the crater and I thought I was going to drown: I didn't know it was a crater, thought it was probably some fucking Falkland loch, probably with monsters in it too. Took me an hour to scramble out.

I couldn't believe my eyes. I'd been plodding along for about three or four hours with my head down, keeping a check for mines, and when I did decide to take a rest and looked up, I could see a telegraph pole. I remember

I started to shake all over. It was very hard to prevent myself from racing over to it, and I had to keep telling myself to be calm. When I finally did reach it, I put my back against it and just slid down on to the ground. Out there with no other sound I could hear the wires humming. Or thought I could. I wanted to anyway, so I did. The shakes started again so I waited for them to shudder themselves out before I stood up. Then I started to follow the wires from pole to pole.

Ages later, many hours, when it was getting dark, I saw lights on the other side of the bay. To get to them meant I had to leave the poles. I was scared to do that. I stood there with my arm around that pole like it was the last friend I had on earth. Then I shook myself and started walking round the bay. The tide was out so I was able to cut off a mile or so.

When I got to the other side I collapsed on to the heather.

I don't think I realised what bad shape I was in until then. When I tried to stand up I couldn't. My legs just wouldn't hold me upright any more. I had to crawl towards the building. The wind started to blow; a dog barked; it sounded like a goddamn wolf to me, really eerie. I kept going forward, afraid that if I stopped I'd never get started again. I didn't care who lived in the farm. Anything they did to me couldn't be worse than what was happening already.

Funny, when I got to the door I couldn't bring myself to knock for a while. I kept thinking, what am I going to say to these people? They'll think I'm something from outer space. Then I thought, bugger it, and banged on the door.

When the door opened the light from inside blinded me for a few seconds. Then I saw it was a woman standing there, wearing only a towel with another smaller towel wrapped round her head like she'd just washed her hair. Of course I thought, Shit, I'm having one of those stupid dreams again. When I found it wasn't a dream I got shocked. I thought, Jesus, they must be right ignorant bastards here letting a woman come to the door like that in the middle of the night. Crazy what gets into your mind at times. Anyway, I started telling her who I was and how I'd got lost.

'Oh yeah. We were told to keep our eye out for a stray,' she said. 'You must be it.'

Ever been made to feel like a bloody sheep?

'You'd better come in,' the woman went on. 'Better take those clothes off too,' she added, and left the room.

I stripped to my underclothes by the fire, and sat down. The woman came back in, dressed. 'I'm Diane Kilmartin,' she told me. 'You're hungry, I suppose.'

'Starving.' And I meant it.

The door banged shut.

'Kevin? Come here,' Diane said. Kevin Kilmartin came in.

'This is Phil Williams,' she told him. 'He's the stray we were supposed to keep an eye out for.'

Kevin looked a bit dazed. 'You're supposed to be dead by now,' he said.

I grinned. 'Well, I'm not, am I?'

'You're supposed to be,' Kevin said again.

'Sorry.'

Later he told me that the war was over. That the Brits had won. That the Scots Guards had already sailed for home. That Spain had won the World Cup. I couldn't have cared less. All I cared about was the beefburgers and beer that Mrs Kilmartin gave me, and the warmth of the fire, and the offer she made of a clean, dry bed.

I didn't get a chance to use the bed though. I looked so sick and shaky Kevin thought it best to call the military. He phoned them on one of those old wind-up machines. I heard him tell whoever was on the other end of the line that he had Philip Williams at his house. And then he kept repeating, Philip Williams. Yes, Philip Williams. Yes, Philip Williams, as though he wasn't being believed. 'They're coming right away,' he said as he put down the phone.

'The lad needs sleep,' said Diane.

'They said they'd be right here.'

I knew why. They were shit scared I might tell someone else about what had happened to me before they got what they wanted out of me. So, I pulled on my wet clothes again, and waited. I'd barely got dressed when we heard the helicopter. I got the shakes again so badly they had to help me into it. All the time an RAF officer was talking at me. I couldn't hear what he was saying above the engine noise, so I ignored him.

The chopper crew led me towards a building with a huge red cross on it, took me inside and down a corridor. They dumped me in front of a nurse sitting behind a desk. Then things started happening quickly.

A doctor appeared. 'Get that man into a bath,' he ordered.

A nurse appeared. 'Come with me,' she said.

The room was bare except for a bath and a chair. The water was already running into the bath. Hot water.

'You have soap and a towel?' the nurse asked, but sounded more like she was telling me.

Oh sure, I thought. Always carry soap and a fucking towel when I'm wandering about this shit-awful country. And, Christ, I thought, how in the name of Jesus do they expect me to have *soap* and a *towel*? 'No,' I told her. 'But I've got a grenade. Will that do?'

She snorted at that and left me, and came back in a while with carbolic soap and a towel. 'Now wash yourself,' she said. 'All over, mind.' And off she went again.

'Hey. Nurse.'

She stuck her head round the door and glared.

'Where am I?'

'What do you mean, where are you?'

'Where am I?'

'Port Stanley.'

'Oh.'

The hot water all over me made me feel quite dizzy. I thought I could feel it seeping right through my pores

58

and collecting inside my skin. I hadn't any energy left after I'd soaped myself down, so I just lay there in the water. I still couldn't believe that I was back among people. I wondered if I'd gone mad and was dreaming again. Another thing I thought was how acute I'd become to sounds and smells after all that time in my own silence and with nothing but the wind and the earth to smell. Doors banging sounded like bombardments. Footsteps in the corridor outside like rifle fire. The rattle of metal dishes on a trolley like tanks rumbling. And because I knew what they really were and not what they sounded like I found them very scary. And the smell of the hospital was weird after all the fresh air. For some reason the antiseptic cleanliness stank like putridness in my nose.

'Haven't you finished?'

It was the nurse again, bustling in, asking her question and going off again without waiting for my answer after putting a clean pair of underpants on the chair.

The next time she appeared I was finished. I was sitting on the edge of the bath feeling very weak. The heat of the bath had drained what little energy I had out of me.

'Right,' the nurse said. 'Come along with me.'

I followed her down the corridor and into the ward I was to share with three others. They were all asleep, one of them snoring. He kept sort of choking and smacking his lips.

'Into bed now,' the nurse said. 'I'll be back in a minute with a nice hot drink for you.'

I don't know if she did come back with a nice hot

drink for me or not. As soon as I hit the bed I was asleep.

Do they always wake you up in hospitals to ask you if you're all right or if you need anything?

Someone was shaking me by the shoulder.

'Are you all right?' a voice with a Dublin accent asked. I opened an eye and saw this big busty nurse looking down at me.

'Do you want anything?'

'Uh-huh,' I grunted.

The big busty nurse with the Dublin accent went off to wake some other poor bastard up.

It was still dark when they woke me again with my breakfast. My eyes were open okay but my brain was still asleep. I started to shake again, and nearly sent the tray flying. I couldn't remember where I was, and for a few minutes I wondered if I'd been captured and was in some sort of prison. It took me almost an hour before I could remember being brought in on the helicopter, and then I had to work through everything slowly to understand where I was and why I was in bed.

None of the other three in the ward said anything to me, nothing to each other either. One was an elderly merchant sailor with a broken leg. The one who'd been snoring was a sailor with his face ripped to bits after a bottle attack. I never found out who the third one was or what was wrong with him.

About noon a bloke called Martin came round and asked me if I wanted anything from the general store.

'Do they have beer?' I asked. I was dying for a beer.

'Sure.'

'And chocolate?'

He looked at me oddly. 'Yeah. They've got chocolate.'

'That'll do me,' I told him. 'Beer and chocolate.'

An hour or so later he came back with cans of beer and a load of chocolate. I noticed his attitude had changed a bit. He was smiling and very friendly. He wouldn't let me pay for the goods either even though I had enough cash, cash I'd carried with me all through the war. He opened one of the cans and handed it to me.

'Ta,' I said.

'You're welcome,' he said. 'Got to treat a star like a star,' he added. That meant nothing to me so I ignored it and took a long swig of beer.

'What's it feel like?' Martin asked.

'What does what feel like?'

'Being news.'

'What d'you mean?'

'You're big news. In all the papers.'

I was very confused. 'Why?'

'Shit. They buried you in England six weeks ago and now you've turned up. That's why.'

I finished my beer and then I got down under the blankets, covering my head. What the fuck did he mean that I'd been buried in England six weeks ago? I started imagining myself in a grave. I felt very cold and started shivering like mad. Then I started to cry. And the awful thing was that I knew I was crying for myself.

It struck me as a bit strange nobody had spoken to me about why I had gone missing at Tumbledown. Maybe, I thought, I was such an insignificant little sod they couldn't have cared less what had become of me. I was wrong.

I was sitting on the edge of my bed, swinging my legs, having a drink and a smoke when a nurse I hadn't seen before came up to me and said there were two personnel officers wanting to see me. I said okay, and she gave me this funny look that said a couple of things: one that I was for it, and the other was that she sympathised.

I followed her down the main corridor and on to this glass porch. It was very pretty, decorated with potted plants and easy chairs covered in bright flowered material. There were two men there. They'd been talking when I came in but stopped immediately they saw me, so I knew they'd had their heads together about me. One of them, a warrant officer, introduced himself. He gave me his rank, his name which I forget, and told me he was a Services Investigation Bureau investigator. The other man also gave me his rank and name which I also forget. It seemed he was there more or less in an advisory capacity: the SIB don't have much knowledge of the practices and methods of soldiering, so this second chap was to explain all that to him if he got confused. Of course there was no one there to explain things to me if *I* got confused.

I honestly can't remember all the things they asked me, but I do recall how it started. The SIB investigator said, 'Right. I want you to tell me exactly what happened

– everything mind – from the eve of Tumbledown right up to when you found yourself in Stanley Hospital.' He started shuffling his papers. Then he said. 'Take your time. I'm going to write every word down. So take your time.'

I happened to look at the clock. It was 3.32 p.m. Five hours later I finished telling him all I could remember. We stopped to stretch and have a smoke. The two of them left me alone and went into a huddle, muttering between themselves.

During all the time I was speaking they never once asked me a question, but when they came back to the table the fun started. Some fun, I can tell you.

The SIB investigator started going through my statement line by line. He wanted details. 'I need the details of that,' he'd say, and just sit there waiting for me to answer. I couldn't give him the fucking details. I'd been out there by myself for seven goddamn weeks and every single day of those seven weeks had been pretty much the same. Or, at least, now that I was back I couldn't remember any differences. I started to feel very frustrated. They had a knack of making me sound stupid. The SIB investigator would put little twists into his voice, making it sound like he was accusing me. Like I was on trial. I could feel myself getting angry. And I got really mad when he started contradicting me. I mean, when I started contradicting myself over some dumb little thing like, say, the weather. If I said it was snowing instead of raining he'd say, 'That's not what you said. You said it was raining, not snowing.'

'What the fuck difference does that make?'

'It makes a lot of difference.'

'Okay. It was snowing *and* frigging raining. Will that do?'

Maybe it was because I was so upset but I was sure they were going to manipulate everything I said and make it look like I deserted instead of getting lost.

At one stage I got up and started stomping about the porch. They just leaned back in their chairs and waited for me to come back and sit down again, like I was a naughty child having a fit of temper.

The main trouble was they wanted everything in neat, strict, military order. But nothing was in neat, strict, military order in my mind. Everything was jumbled up. Everything piled on top of one another in a heap. I couldn't separate the days of those seven weeks like the SIB investigator wanted me to. I could hardly remember what had happened to me yesterday, let alone all that while ago.

Finally he seemed satisfied. He passed me the statement. I signed my name on page after page after page. I remember near the end WILLIAMS was just about a straight line. Except the very last page. I signed that with great care. I don't know why.

He gathered up the papers and tapped them on the table to make sure they were all neatly stacked. Then the two of them got up and walked out without a word, leaving me sitting there.

I felt giddiness coming over me and wondered what I'd done. Maybe I'd signed my life away. Maybe I was going to be shot. I know that sounds daft now, but at the time it was really scary.

It was exactly 3 a.m.

The same nurse who had taken me there came back to escort me back to bed. She gave me a hot drink and a sleeping pill. She gave me a little hug too, and said something about my not to worry about those nasty men. Frightened though I was I had to giggle at that. I could see it made her happy that she'd made me cheer up.

The pill soon made me drowsy. It was a relief to be alone.

NINE

They kept me in Stanley Hospital for two weeks. During that time nobody else spoke to me about the fact that I'd been missing. In fact, everyone seemed to avoid the subject. Maybe they sensed something was going to blow up, and they thought there was a chance it might go away if they ignored it. All I really knew was what Martin told me and I don't know if that was true: that they were worried they'd be accused of not looking for me properly.

The Scots Guards were well out at sea now, so they told me I was to be flown to Ascension. When the day for that came I had to put on my combat clothing again. It hadn't been cleaned. Just rolled up and shoved somewhere. Jesus, it really stank. There were even patches of mould on it.

The flight took twelve hours. We refuelled in the sky and that, I can tell you, was very impressive. I sat beside a colonel who was very friendly, although he did start off by sniffing a lot at the smell I created. He was about sixty and kept showing me photographs of his wife. She was young and very pretty. I think conquering her meant more to him than beating the Argies. I think that if I'd got her I'd have felt the same.

On landing in Ascension I was met by a couple of Transport Regiment staff. I was to billet with them in a large villa, empty except for camp beds and fridges. I was told I was to be there for a week, and was issued with jungle combat gear, and was told to relax.

It was like being in heaven. The weather was great, sunny and warm. I could lounge on the beaches as much as I wanted, and there were plenty of duty-free bars. I messed about a bit with a St Helena girl, and drank a lot.

All the time, though, I was thinking, What's the catch? There's got to *be* a catch. The Army don't treat you like this unless there *is* a catch.

And still no one mentioned the Falklands to me. No one in authority, I mean. The other soldiers billeted there had other things to talk about. They were all fed up with the Falklands as a subject for conversation. Most of them, like me, wished they'd never seen the place. The thing that seemed to annoy them most apparently was how the Falkland Islanders kept complaining about them – once they'd saved the bloody place, of course.

I was quite sorry when the ship carrying the Scots Guards pulled into Ascension. The US Air Force had plenty of grass and they were very generous with it. I knew I'd have to cut that out for a while when the ship came to anchor about half a mile off shore.

They flew me out to the ship by helicopter and our colonel immediately briefed and debriefed me. He smiled a lot and seemed perfectly happy with the way things went. He shook my hand and welcomed me back, and patted me on the shoulder.

Then I was debriefed by Sergeant Morcom. He grabbed me on one of the corridors and pulled me into a cabin. 'You're a right daft cunt, you are. Getting lost, for shit's sake,' he said. Then he gave me my backlog of mail. There was a parcel: chocolate, cigarettes and things. Alison had enclosed some Kendal mint cake and a pair of sexy red briefs. Fuck me, I thought, did she expect me to wear them on the Falklands? I got really annoyed with those briefs for a while. Somehow they showed me how little people in England knew about what had gone on. Like I was off on holiday or something. Then I calmed down and thought it was really pretty nice of people to send me anything at all.

I thought we would all be going home on the ship. Not so. We were flown back to England by jet. I was told to sit up front. 'We want you to be last off,' someone said, but didn't say why.

We landed at Brize Norton and everyone started to pile off. Everyone, that is, except for me. 'Wait,' I was told. Then, 'Right, you can get off now.' I went down the steps. The Duke of Kent was waiting there. He said something, something nice I suppose, as I saluted, but I couldn't tell what it was. Being isolated like I was, I was feeling nervous and suspicious and frightened. A couple of officers led me into a huge concrete building. There were people in uniform hurrying everywhere. I thought they kept looking at me out of the corner of their eyes, but maybe I imagined that. The officers kept talking to me like they were trying to explain something, but I was feeling completely lost and couldn't seem to make sense out of their words.

They opened a door and told me to go in, following me. The room was quite small and bare. There were some people standing round. They all came up to me in turn and hugged me and kissed me and said things into my ear. I know now it was Mam and Dad and the rest of my family, and Alison, but I swear to God, for some queer reason, I hadn't a clue who they were at the time. I mean, I knew I knew them, but my mind wouldn't relate them to me.

One of the officers stepped forward and said something like, 'Will you all please come with me?' and we all followed him back down the corridor and out of another door.

There must have been at least a hundred press photographers there. And reporters who kept shouting at me, trying to get me to perform. I was terrified. I turned and started to run back into the building. The officer caught up with me and took me by the arm. 'I think we better go along with this,' he said, making it clear that this was an order. 'Just give them what they want and things will be easier,' he added.

Things started moving in a sort of slow motion. I was being pushed here and there and the flashbulbs were flashing. And people were being shoved up beside me and told to put their arms around me and the flashbulbs flashed some more. I was having questions shouted at me and I could hear myself making answers but the answers I gave didn't seem to fit what was asked. I kept having the feeling that all I wanted was to sit down somewhere that was noiseless and green. I don't know why I wanted it green. I just did.

Anyway, eventually it was over. The officer said, 'Now, that wasn't so bad, was it?' I'd have loved to have kicked him right in the balls.

We were bundled into coaches for the drive to Chelsea. Nobody spoke to me on the journey. Nobody seemed to want to sit beside me either. Fuck them, then, I said to myself, and stared and stared out of the window, seeing nothing.

The band of the Grenadier Guards were playing in the square. Everyone was very jolly, laughing and horsing around. We were to be paid off and sent on six weeks' leave. It came to my turn to be paid and I wasn't on the paylist. You don't put dead people on the paylist, you see. I stood there like a fool as they muttered about what they were going to do: without the right paperwork they were all in a heap. Paperwork was the battery that kept their minds working, I suppose. Anyway, in the end, rather than be made look really stupid, they gave me a thousand pounds, guessing that that was about what I had coming.

The sergeant major took me to one side. 'Now you

go home with your parents and stay at home, son,' he said. 'It's been arranged that you have regular visits from a military PR from Preston. He'll handle the press for you, so you'll have nothing to worry about. Just remember, say nothing to anyone unless the PR approves. Nothing, understand?'

I said I understood, but I hadn't a clue what he was talking about. Why would the press be bothering me?

I was given a large malt whisky and dismissed for my six weeks of leave.

TEN

The journey up the M1 and M6 was monotonous, but it was also like a fantasy. I sat in the back, my Dad drove, my Mam beside him. Mam kept turning her head round to talk to me but, although I knew she was just being kind, her continuous flow of chatter bugged me. It all seemed so stupid. So bloody petty really. Yak, yak, yak about nothing. All I wanted was to be left alone. I'd started getting headaches and when I had them I kept thinking about my seven weeks alone. Nobody'd bothered about me then, so what was the big deal now?

Why I came out with it I don't know, but I said, 'I think I'll take a holiday. Spain, maybe. I've got a thousand quid.'

Mam went berserk. 'You'll do no such thing,' she said. 'You'll stay right at home like you were told. Besides, it's time you thought about us. We haven't seen you in ages. You owe it to us to stay at home for a while.'

I didn't say anything to that. I wanted to say that I

didn't think I owed anyone anything right now, but I didn't.

I got another shock when we arrived in Halton and turned into the road where my parents lived. It was crowded with people all laughing and clapping and peering into the car at me.

'What the hell is going on, Mam?'

'They're here to welcome you home.'

'Jesus, I don't want them here.'

'Don't be so ungrateful.'

The garden wall was covered with a huge sheet of white something, and on it was written WELCOME HOME. WELL DONE PHIL. The front of the house was draped in a gigantic Union Jack.

I pulled myself out of the car. It was like I was Michael Jackson or somebody. Everyone wanting to touch me and shake my hand, patting me on the back and telling me how great I was. I couldn't understand it. In one way I was pleased they cared, but I couldn't understand what they cared about, if that makes sense.

The house was packed too. With relatives. I never knew I had so many. They all hugged me and kissed me, and half the women were crying. Someone gave me a bottle of champagne, so I took a swig. It tasted okay so I drank the lot. Everyone cheered at that. 'Good old Phil,' they said. Yeah, I thought, good old Phil.

It should have been a hell of a party. I think it probably was for everyone else. I wanted to get lost someplace and be on my own. I tried to explain this to Mam, but she told me not to be so silly. So I said to hell with it and got drunk and fell asleep.

Mam woke me for breakfast. I didn't feel like eating but it was so long since I'd had a fry-up I couldn't resist it. All the time I was eating Mam was telling me how much she'd missed me even if I was difficult to put up with. When I'd finished eating I said, 'I'm going out.'

'You better not, Phil,' Mam said.

'Why not?'

'The reporters.'

'What reporters?'

'Go look out of the window.'

They were there all right. About six car loads. Waiting. I suddenly got very depressed and went upstairs and lay down on the bed. Mam followed me up in a little while. 'What do they want, Mam?'

'The reporters? To talk to you, of course. You're famous, Phil,' she told me and sounded quite proud.

'Why?'

'Why? Don't be so silly.'

Mam never did understand that I hadn't a clue why everyone was so interested in me all of a sudden.

I didn't go out of the house for the next couple of days. I knew I was getting depressed but couldn't do anything about it. I kept playing 'Radio K.A.O.S.' by Roger Waters. That helped me for a while, particularly when he sang 'But oh the tide is turning'. Unfortunately it wasn't turning for me, though.

That song always made me think of something that happened on Ascension. Myself and a couple of Royal Corps of Transport soldiers went to a local bar for some beers. There were some local people there with their kids. One little girl, about three years old, came over and climbed on to my knee. I was so shattered by the fact that she wasn't afraid of me, that she didn't give a damn who I was or what I was or what had happened to me that I burst out crying. I sat there for ages cuddling her, the tears streaming down my face like a right pillock. So, listening to the song made me think of that, and made me think things like, I hope those kids never have to get involved in a stupid bloody war. And then, in my mind, I'd see them dead and burning, and that would make me start crying again.

Mam thought I was crying because I was so happy to be home. I heard her telling the neighbours that I was coming out of things fine.

ELEVEN

I think I better go back a bit now, and tell you what had been going on at home while I was wandering about the bogs of the Falklands. It'll help you understand what all the fuss was about, which is more than I did at the time.

When Martin told me in the hospital that I'd been buried six weeks earlier he was exaggerating a bit as you might have guessed. But they had had a memorial service for me in the local church. Yeah, that's right, the Army had sent some halfwitted captain to tell my parents I was dead. Mam told me about it. Not willingly; I had to drag it out of her. I think she thought she was tempting some sort of fate by mentioning it.

'It was awful, Phil,' Mam said. 'I was tidying up and your Dad was sitting there with his feet in a bowl of water, when the captain came to the door. He was all embarrassed and wouldn't look at us as he spoke. He just said that you'd been lost in the battle on Mount Tumbledown. He said they'd been looking for you but hadn't found your body. So they assumed you'd been killed. He said there were nine other soldiers killed with you like that was supposed to make us feel better.'

'Go on.'

'Nothing more. That was that. He left after that to tell the other families of their losses, I suppose.'

'What then?' I asked.

Then the letters started arriving, it seemed. Official ones confirming my tragic demise. Poor old me. Dead as a dodo. The first one was this:

Colonel J A Dunsmure, OBE
Lieutenant Colonel Commanding
Scots Guards
Wellington Barracks
Birdcage Walk
London, SW1E 6HQ
22 June 1982

Dear Mr and Mrs Williams,

It is with the deepest sorrow that I write this letter to you about your son who is missing and most unfortunately must be presumed to have died in the final battle for Port Stanley.

I understand from his commanding officer to whom I spoke yesterday that they have made a thorough search before filing him as missing.

I am well aware that letters like mine can only offer the heartfelt sympathy of the whole Regiment in the hope that this can be of some comfort to you and to his sister [sic].

In the longer term I hope that you will let me know if there is anything the Regiment can do to help you or your family.

Yours sincerely
James Dunsmure   Colonel

My Mam was really pleased with this one. She thought how nice the Colonel must be to sit down and write her a letter in his own hand, and not having someone type it. Of course she didn't know at the time what a load of bullshit it really was. I mean, to begin with, why tell her that a thorough search had been made for me when it hadn't? I know he *had* to say that but why put it in writing? I know the Scots Guards. They're very thorough in everything they do, and if, like he told my Mam, a thorough search had been made they'd have found me no bother. I'm not saying they thought, 'Fuck Williams. He's not worth looking for.' I'm sure they had the odd peep around the place, but sure as hell they didn't put themselves out. The way I've always figured it is that if I could find them they should certainly have been able to find little me if they'd tried even halfway hard.

Then the bit about letting him know if there was anything the bloody Regiment could do to help. Christ, he'd have shit himself if Mam did ask for any help. He probably guessed Mam would be too proud to ask for help of any kind, and anyway, as we were to find out, they only offered the help because they thought I was dead, and there's not a lot of help a dead man needs, is there?

Actually, this great military generosity was the theme of nearly all the letters that arrived. But once they'd written and done their noble little bit, they never bothered about Mam and Dad again. All they wanted, I think, was to have on record how concerned and thoughtful they were, and I'm sure there were a lot of parents conned in the same way. Most of them were probably working class like mine, and they'd have been pretty dazzled by all the flashy letter headings. Probably intimidated by it, too.

A couple of days after Colonel Dunsmure wrote the big guns took a hand, not wanting to be left out, I suppose, in case someone thought they were uncaring.

> *Lieutenant General Sir Richard Trant KCB*
> *Headquarters South East District*
> *Aldershot Hants GU11 2DP*

Mrs R Williams
Halton
Lancaster
Lancs

> *24 June 1982*

Dear Mrs Williams,
It is with the deepest sorrow that I heard of the loss of your son whilst his Battalion was serving with 5th Infantry Brigade, a formation of my command.

You will, I know, have heard or be hearing from the Army Board and the Regiment and they will offer you every assistance.

Please accept my wife's and my personal condolences. Our prayers as a family are with every member of the Task Force — they go with you especially in your sorrow.

Yours sincerely,
Richard Trant

Lancaster City Council
Mayor's Parlour
Town Hall
Lancaster LA1 1PJ

Mr and Mrs A Williams,
Halton
Lancaster

25 June 1982

Dear Mr and Mrs Williams,

I have just learnt with sorrow of the death of your son Philip in the Falkland Islands Conflict.

The pride that has come to everyone from the success of the Task Force is certainly tempered with the knowledge of the sacrifice that this success has entailed, particularly when one of the casualties is a son of Lancaster.

Please know that the Mayoress and I, together with

*all the citizens of Lancaster share your loss and your
grief with you.*

Yours sincerely,
Geoffrey Bryan
Mayor

Wow! The Mayor and his lady wife. That was something.
But if you thought that was terrific, how about this one
from the House of Commons, no less.

> *House of Commons*
> *London SW1A 0AA*

Mr and Mrs C A Williams,
Halton,
Lancaster.

> *24 June 1982*

Dear Mr and Mrs Williams,
    I was desperately sorry to read in today's Telegraph
that your son is feared to have been lost.
    *It is always sad, but particularly so when the action
was so nearly at an end, and you believed he was safe.*
    *If there is anything at all I can do to help, please let
me know.*
    *I hope that your friends will be able to bring you a
measure of comfort.*

Yours with sympathy,
Elaine Kellett-Bowmac

All that was needed now was something from Buck Palace itself and we'd have been rightly made up.

Now before you all start thinking what a shit I am for being so ungrateful, let me say that I *know* these people meant well, even if they were only fulfilling some sort of obligation. I'm sure they meant exactly what they said, thinking that when they'd written it would all be over and done with. But when I popped up again, alive and kicking, it made them look like right wallies, and they hated that. And you can't blame them. But why they had to take it out on me and my family I'll never understand. It was as if we, and not the Army, had made the cock-up.

Anyway, I've saved the prize until last. When I read it now it really amazes me that a supposedly intelligent human being can actually think such bullshit. It just shows, I guess, how really thick those in power think us ordinary people are. I suppose I should feel a bit sorry for the poor sod. All the way through his letter you can see him madly trying to justify to himself the fucking Falklands even though he must have seen, like we all did, that it was pointless, stupid and nothing more than a frigging exercise in someone's megalomania. And apart from that the information he was officially transmitting was totally wrong, although it was really nice to know that I'd died alongside my comrades in a famous regiment (sorry, Regiment). That makes a pretty picture, doesn't it? There's me, riddled with Argie bullets, gasping my last, and the famous Regiment gathered about, singing goddamn hymns, I suppose, and seeing me off to that great barracks in the sky. Anyway, here's the letter. Judge for yourself.

> Major General H D A Langley MBE
> Headquarters
> Household Division
> Horse Guards
> Whitehall
> London SW1A 2AX

Mrs R Williams
Halton
Lancaster
Lancs

> 26 June 1982

Dear Mr and Mrs Williams,

I am so desperately sorry about the tragic death of your son in the last hours of fighting in the Falkland Islands and offer you and your family my very deepest sympathy in your great loss.

The engagement fought by the 2nd Bn Scots Guards, on Tumbledown Mountain was vital to the successful capture of Port Stanley. The opposition was tough and it took all the Scots Guards' skill and bravery to win. But war is always sad and saddest for those whose loved ones are killed.

Nothing that I can say can reduce your grief or sense of loss, but I do ask you to believe that in giving his life in the service of his country and thus depriving *you of his love and companionship, it was in no sense a waste.*

Firstly the cause he was fighting for was a just one. It was to resist unprovoked aggression and restore their freedom to people of British stock. Secondly he was doing his duty which is what a soldier's life is about: thirdly he died alongside his comrades in a famous Regiment taking part in a historic and victorious campaign.

You have cause to be very proud of him and must remember him always as a brave Scots Guardsman.

Yours sincerely
Major General Desmond Langley

So now, definitely and officially, I was dead. No room for doubt.

'A few days later,' Mam told me, 'someone rang up and said – he said it would be quite appropriate – that was his word, I remember – appropriate to hold a memorial service for you.'

'Wow!' I said, for no particular reason.

'Three hundred people came to it, Phil,' Mam went on. 'Imagine! Three hundred. The church was packed. We put up a memorial to you in the porch. There was a big photograph of you – a coloured one – and a Bible, and a single red rose.'

'What for? Why the rose?'

'Lancaster. And I thought it would be nice.'

'Oh.'

'And they sent a Scots Guards piper to play the lament.'

'Lovely.'

'And an army captain read the lesson.'

'Great.'

'And a bugler played the Last Post.'

'Terrific.'

'Oh, it was lovely, Phil.'

'Must have been.'

'I know you'd have loved it.'

I was going to say something nasty to that, but I changed my mind. Mam only meant it nicely. She hadn't a clue what it was doing to me.

'We put a tribute in the local paper too.

> They say that time kills sorrow,
> For some that may be true.
> No morning dawns or night returns
> But still we think of you.

. . . That's what it said.'

To be absolutely honest I wanted to puke when I heard that. It was so corny and phoney. We'd never *really* got on that well, my parents and me, and to hear Mam say they'd be thinking of me at dawn and night sounded a bit like she was taking the piss.

I said, 'That was really nice, Mam.'

'And you know what the heading for the report of the service was?'

'Tell me.'

'A Hero Laid to Rest. That's what it said.'

'They got the laid bit right.'

'What do you mean, Phil?'

'Nothing.'

'And there were two photographs. That nice one of you in uniform standing in front of the armoured car — you know, that one we have over the telly.'

'Oh, the portrait of a fascist?'

'Don't be silly. And one of Piper Sergeant Donald Macleod and Bugler Corporal Tom Dodd outside the church.'

'Pretty, were they?'

'Very smart they looked in dress uniforms.'

'I'll bet.'

'And in big print it said, TRIBUTES TO TEENAGER WHO DIED FOR BRITAIN.'

Rousing stuff, wasn't it?

The one really daft thing my parents did was to go and see a medium. I know they were upset and everything but, Christ, you'd think they'd have more sense than to go to a bloody medium. A right con it was as far as I can make out. The trouble was Mam was uneasy because they'd never actually found my body. She kept telling herself that *maybe* I was still alive. I suppose some idiot had told her not to worry because since I hadn't been found I *might* turn up, meaning it nicely and all, and Mam latched on to that without thinking. As it happened she was right, but at the time nothing would satisfy her but to consult this medium. So, on her

Philip in his Scots Guards uniform, shortly after enlisting.
(Times Newspapers Ltd)

Outside the Falklands army field hospital, supported by nurses Lieutenant Corporal Liz Jones and Captain Judy Gorrod, 3 August 1982. (Press Association)

Reunited with Mam and Dad, 10 August 1982. (Press Association)

Above: With Alison, the same day. (Press Association) *Right*: A staged photograph of Philip, just after his return. (Press Association) *Below*: The Williams family: (l-r) Angela, Dad, Karen, Alison, Philip, Gareth, Mam, and Cherith. (Press Association)

During the filming of *Resurrected*, with David Thewlis, the actor who played Philip. (Philip Williams)

(Times Newspapers Ltd)

birthday, my Dad drove her south to see Doris Stokes. Some birthday present!

Now, I know old Doris is dead, and I don't like saying anything nasty about dead people who can't defend themselves, but Doris must really have seen my Mam coming, and had the time of her life conning her. As far as I can make out the chat went something like this:

'I have news for you, dear,' Doris said when she came back from her trip to the other world.

Mam waited.

'Your Phil is in Goose Green.'

'Oh no,' Mam said. 'He was lost on Tumbledown. The army told us that.'

Old Doris didn't give a shit what the Army said. 'Never mind what they told you, dear,' she insisted. 'He's in Goose Green.' Well, she could hardly change her story *that* quickly, could she? I mean, it would be pretty galling to be caught on her very first bit of inspired crap. So she stuck to her guns. 'Definitely Goose Green.' Then she said the thing that *I* think was horrible. She said, 'I think he might be alive.'

She *thought* I *might* be alive, for fuck sake. Shit, that was covering her tracks for sure. And supposing I had been dead? I know I wasn't, but supposing I had been? Then my Mam would have spent the rest of her life hearing that stupid old fraud hinting that I might be alive. And what would *that* have done to my Mam? Made her as cracked as old Doris, most likely. And you'll understand the wicked impression Stokes made on Mam when I tell you that as they were driving back up the motorway the back door of the car gave a little click and opened. It wouldn't enter Mam's head that they just hadn't shut it properly and that the wind forced it open. Oh, no. Doris had got her into a right state. 'That was our Phil getting into the car,' she told Dad. 'Our Phil hitching a ride.' And she really believed that for ages. Even Dad must have been a bit intimidated because he never tried to stop her thinking those daft things.

One other thing: just so you won't start believing all the military were in deepest mourning for me, this arrived to cheer Mam up:

> *Director General of Defence Accounts*
> *Ministry of Defence*
> *Whittington Road Worcester WR5 2LA*

Mrs R Williams
Halton
Lancaster
Lancashire

> *5 July 1982*

Dear Mrs Williams
THE LATE GUARDSMAN P. A. WILLIAMS — 2 SCOTS GUARDS
  I apologise for troubling you with matters of a business nature so soon after the death of your son but feel you may want to have some idea of the action

which will need to be taken to settle his service affairs.

I am therefore writing to advise you that it is the responsibility of my Branch of the Ministry of Defence to distribute assets due from Service sources to the estates of personnel who die while serving.

I should explain that matters of a Service nature affecting an estate are firstly dealt with by a Committee of Adjustment set up at the deceased's unit but cannot be settled completely until full information has been received from the accounting authorities concerned regarding any outstanding pay and allowances due to the estate or any charges due from the estate. When all this information is available and the Committee of Adjustment's report has been received, I will send a full statement to you.

You will also wish to know that my Branch will authorise the release of any personal effects held in Service custody as soon as it is possible to establish who is entitled to receive them.

If there are solicitors acting in connection with the estate, will you please be good enough to inform this office of their name and address and, if you so wish, future correspondence will be conducted with them. You are advised that if you do decide to employ solicitors to act on your behalf, the cost must be borne by yourself. You may of course prefer to postpone any decision about whether to engage solicitors until you have received full details of the sums due to the estate from all sources (ie from not only the Ministry of Defence but from other organisations such as Banks, Building Societies, Insurance Companies etc).

Yours sincerely
B. Brooks

Just the sort of thing grieving parents need to get, it was. And it came before they'd had time to have their little memorial service and all. For me it proved just how thick and ignorant officialdom was. Not that I was supposed to know, of course. I was 'the late' by them.

TWELVE

'It was almost worse than them coming to tell us you were dead,' Mam told me.

'Thanks a lot,' I said, trying to make a bit of a joke, and cheer her up.

We were talking about when the colonel from the local garrison came to say I had turned up, and was alive.

'He was standing on the doorstep, hopping from foot to foot, with a great big smile on his face,' Mam went on, not getting my attempt at a joke, or not hearing it. 'He made me very angry, Phil. I wanted to shout at him and tell him to stop looking so happy because, you see, you were still a bit dead in my head even if this officer was saying you were alive. He didn't seem to care at all about what we'd been through.'

'Well, he wouldn't, would he?'

'Well, he should have. He should at least have said he was sorry for the mistake – not just standing there grinning and expecting me to get all delighted and grateful. I kept thinking, it's all right. They're making another mistake. Our Phil really is dead.'

I could relate to that all right. 'I can understand that, Mam,' I told her.

'Then I wanted to hit him,' Mam continued. 'I wanted to hit him for telling us you were dead in the first place without being absolutely sure, and putting us through everything, and then for just thinking that by coming and smiling and telling us you'd turned up alive everything would be back to normal.'

'You should have. Hit him,' I told Mam.

Mam smiled, knowing I knew she'd never do such a thing. She'd clout us kids okay, but not a stranger.

I think that what worried Mam and Dad most was that they felt they'd been made to look like fools, as if somehow *they* were responsible for the Army cock-up, as if they'd put out the story that I was dead. I mean, they're very working class and all that, but they have feelings and they're very respectable. And now someone had come and turned everything upside down again just when they were getting used to the idea that I wouldn't be around, making *them* look like liars.

'It was like everything had been a dreadful mockery, Phil. All of us crying and praying for you at the service.'

Bastard that I am, I had to have a bit of a laugh at that. I could imagine what it must have been like. Like the social event of the decade, that's what. All the neighbours out in their best clothes – some had even got new hats, I heard, just like for a wedding; all trying to get the best seats, all hoping to get a mention or their photograph in the paper. Maybe you think I'm really ungrateful and am making that up, but I'm not, as you'll hear later.

So, I could certainly understand Mam's feelings about the colonel. She couldn't sleep for days, she told me, worrying that the neighbours would think she and Dad had invented the whole thing for some mad reason, and they'd be furious that they'd got all dressed up for nothing. And she was right. There are still some people who won't talk to Mam and Dad, and that shatters Mam, although Dad doesn't give a damn. 'Better off without them,' is what he says. But Mam's still hurt.

'And another thing, Phil. I thought everyone would be so happy for me when I told them you were alive. But lots weren't. They gave me strange looks like I'd known all along you'd survived, and they snapped their words at me curtly.'

'Fuck them, Mam,' I said.

'Mind your language, Phil,' Mam said.

I told you she was respectable.

So that's the scene I came home to: Mam and Dad and the rest of the family delighted, but a bit scared too that I was back. The thing that sticks in my mind is the way they all kept trying to touch me, hugging and kissing me, or just putting a hand on me like they were reassuring themselves I was truly there.

And you might have thought what a lovely, friendly place I lived in when I told you how everyone turned out in force to see me come home. Well, that's all it was — to see me. To see the freak. I can see a crowd of them gawping at me as if I might be a ghost. Oh, I can hear you now, saying, Jesus, what an arrogant, ungrateful bastard he is. Maybe I am. But how do you explain that after a couple of days very few people wanted to talk to me, and kept averting their eyes from me, and some of them even crossing the road so as not to meet me? Maybe they thought I would contaminate them with my spookiness, but I believe they'd decided to teach me and Mam and Dad a lesson for misleading them.

Funny, isn't it, how some people, people you'd never suspect, can enjoy being cruel?

'Why don't the two of you go out for a drink?' Mam would suggest to Dad and me. We'd look at each other and know we both wanted to go but that we were both afraid of the discomfort of everybody staring and whispering about us. So, Dad would say, 'There's something on the telly I want to see.'

And I'd say: 'No, it's nice here at home,' even though home was driving me crazy and making me feel like I was in prison.

And Mam would say, 'As long as you're happy,' knowing neither of us were.

And, once, Mam said, 'I can't look at you without thinking you're dead, Phil.'

'Maybe I am.'

'Don't say things like that.'

'No. Really. Maybe I am.' It was my way of telling her that the Phil who had gone away really *was* dead. Although they couldn't see it yet I knew I had changed so much that something of me was dead. And it was something of me that I'd liked, so that made it worse.

'You're not the same,' Alison told me.
   'Sure I am.'
   'No you're not.'
   'Okay, I'm not. Big deal.'
That was another thing that depressed me and made me very nervous. Everyone expecting me to be the same as I used to be. Expecting someone like me to be sent off to war at seventeen, and be shot at, and see dead bodies lying rotten everywhere, and get lost, and be really scared, and feel yourself going a bit mad at times, and imagining horrors because you couldn't control your mind, and to come back just the same easy-going chap you were.

Sure, Alison was right when she said I was different, but at that stage I was still trying to pretend, even to myself, that I wasn't.

You see, the way I was figuring it was if I *was* the same then all that had happened to me meant nothing. That's to say my mind hadn't been all fucked up and I'd be able to fit in again like people wanted. But if I was *different* then I'd been messed up, and because I still couldn't understand in what way I'd been screwed, I was frightened.

BOOK TWO

THIRTEEN

You remember I told you the headline in the papers when they thought I was dead: A HERO LAID TO REST. Well, after I got home they came up with another one, a real beauty: ALIVE! FALKLANDS BATTLE HERO GIVEN UP FOR DEAD IS BACK. That was the *Daily Mail*. A week later the *Daily Express* had a picture of me being welcomed off the plane by the Duke of Kent. A ROYAL WELCOME FOR LOST SOLDIER, that one said.

I simply couldn't understand what all this hero crap was about. I just got lost, that was all. I'd been cold and hungry and shit scared. I couldn't see anything very heroic in all that. And since the Army hadn't let the reporters question me, they made up things. Real crap, like how I'd eaten worms to stay alive. Shit, it was so fucking cold and the ground so hard the sodding worms had their own troubles trying to survive. I never even saw one, let alone ate one. I'm surprised none of them thought to say I had a bit of roast Argie and cabbage to keep me going.

I hadn't been home on leave all that long when the PR man from Preston came to call. I think even he was surprised at the number of pressmen hanging around the house. I'm sure he'd never faced anything like that before.

'We better give them *something* to keep them quiet,' he said, like he was going to dish out bits of me as souvenirs.

'Like what?'

'A few photos to satisfy them.'

'Christ, more photos. Didn't they get enough at Brize Norton? They've being doing nothing but take photos since I got back.'

'Yes. Well, they want more.'

'Shit!'

'I think you better. I know them. They'll just stay there until they get what they want.'

'Oh, all right.'

'That's better.' He cheered up so much that I wondered if he was getting a commission on all the photos. 'But remember,' he went on, 'nothing about the Falklands. You can answer questions about anything else but not the Falklands. Clear?'

'Very clear.'

'Good,' he said and smiled at me again.

They trundled me off to the river. The press had decided, Christ knows why, that'd be nice to have their Falklands Hero fishing. They made me pose in all sorts of ways, like I was a pop singer or something. And they kept firing questions at me. They came so fast at me I didn't have time to get the answers out, so in the end I ignored them and let the PR do the talking. Then they wanted a picture of me in the local pub, looking jolly having a pint, real crap stuff that would make it seem I was relaxed and having a great time. Luckily the PR said no to that before I exploded.

'That's enough for now,' he said and walked with me back home again. I didn't know it, and I don't think the PR did, but that was a big mistake. We both learned pretty quick that if the press didn't get what they wanted they'd make it up.

Within a couple of days the articles and photographs started appearing again. It seemed they just couldn't get enough of me. They'd even dug up one of me being supported by two nurses while I was recuperating in the hospital in Port Stanley. I looked a right prat in that one. I looked even worse in the one they called KISS OF A LIFETIME FOR HERO BACK FROM THE DEAD. That was Alison and me supposedly in a passionate embrace. Our noses were all jambed up against each other, and from the look on her face you'd swear I'd been chewing garlic or something. I don't even remember having it taken. It was just one of the hundreds I was conned into posing for. I suppose it was meant to cover the romantic angle.

On 11 August, beside a photograph of me and my family in a group, all of us obligingly smiling, the *Manchester Evening News*, without reason, printed the headline, A DESERTER? NOT ME, SAYS SOLDIER. I'd never said anything about deserting. I'd never even been asked anything about deserting and the word desertion had not been mentioned since my debriefing in the Falklands. But they decided it would make a sensational headline; they didn't give a toss what it would do to me.

That's the cruel thing about the papers. They print what they like about somebody and that person has very little comeback. It's a bit like the judge telling the jury to ignore something they've just heard, only with newspapers it's worse. People believe what they read. Maybe it's because they want to believe it or maybe it's because they are too dumb to sift the lies from the truth – not that they can be blamed for that. The papers are supposed to tell the truth, aren't they?

Anyway, there must be a lot of nutcases who read the *Manchester Evening News*, because during the next few weeks they came out from under their stones and had a right go at me.

FOURTEEN

You can always tell whem Mam is really upset. She clamps this smile on her face and keeps it there like her lips were stuck.

'What's up, Mam?' I asked.

Mam put the bundle of letters on the table. A lot of nice people had been writing to me, saying that they were glad I was back safe, and how proud England was of me. I'd asked Mam to read all my letters. They worried me, even though they were kind. I felt I shouldn't be getting them, that I'd done nothing spectacular. It was only the papers making out that I had.

'More letters?'

'Yes,' Mam said. 'Horrible ones.'

She wasn't joking. Suddenly, because of the snide remark in that Manchester rag, I *was* a deserter, to some people anyway. One letter said I should be shot. Another said I should have my balls ripped off. Another, really sad, said I should have died instead of their son. None were signed, of course. Oddly enough I felt nothing as I read those letters. It was like they weren't really for me, but were just another part of the crazy dream I was living through.

Then the phonecalls started, nearly always at night when they knew we'd be trying to sleep. It's really creepy to hear a voice on the phone tell you that he's waiting to kill you. With the number of threats I got there must have been a regiment of them out there waiting to gun me down. One moron that called sounded really sinister. He wanted to chat with me, he said, before he blew the shit out of me.

'Fine,' I said. 'What d'you want to chat about?'

'About you, you fucking traitor,' he said.

'Why call me a traitor?'

''Cause that's what you fucking are.'

'How do you know that?'

'I read all about you in the paper.'

'You must be right thick if you believe everything you read in the paper,' I told him.

He went crazy at that, calling me things I'd never heard of. 'Just let me see you in the pub,' he said, 'and you're dead.'

'Great,' I told him. 'I'm going there tonight. See you.'

And that evening I went down to the local, and sat there for about three hours waiting. I really wanted to see what such a nutter looked like – I was looking forward to meeting him. Mind you, I did have a sheath knife down the leg of my trousers. I may have been going out of my head but I wasn't daft enough to let some half-cocked mental case kill me without putting up some sort of defence. Naturally, he never showed.

There was a kind of funny side to it too, though. It wasn't so great at the time, but looking back and thinking about it, I can't help laughing. I actually got some dirty phonecalls. Women ringing me up and saying they'd never had it off with a coward and telling me how they'd do it with me. Bloody hell, some of the positions sounded worse than the frigging obstacle course. Some didn't speak at all, the usual, just groaned and moaned and panted. There was one very strange one, I remember. Some woman wanted me to give her a baby to replace the son she'd lost. Why she wanted me I never could figure out. Of course I don't know if she'd lost a son either. She could have been making that up, so my sadness for her might have been wasted. The weirdest one was the woman who wanted one of my boots. She went on and on about the smell of leather and foot-sweat – the things she was going to do with my bloody boot were quite amazing. I never told my Mam about this. She'd have died if I did. I never told her either that my underpants were in huge demand. Three women wanted them. One woman even offered me fifty quid if I'd send her the pair I'd worn during the time I was lost, saying things like I must have wanked myself off in them and she'd really like to have a sniff. I couldn't believe she really thought I might still have them. Maybe she thought I'd had them framed and had them hung up in the sitting room. A lovely picture they would have made. I was a bit tempted to make a pair up for her, get them really grotty – you know, piss and crap in them. The fifty quid would have been useful. She even gave me an address but I don't know if it existed. I should have tried to find out, I'd really like to see what a freak like that looked like. I bet her husband didn't know what she was up to, and I know she had a husband since she mentioned right at the beginning that he didn't turn her on any more. I'm not surprised. It'd be hard for him if she needed to get her kicks out of *my* dirty knickers.

While it was all right for me getting those calls, it was a different matter for Mam. I told her not to answer the phone when she was alone, but she always would, in case it was important, she said. The freaks always kept the really frightening stuff for her, telling her they were going to blow up the house like that shitty son of hers should have been blown up. Or that they were going to shoot *her* the next time they saw her leaving the house. It got so Mam was really scared to go out, thinking there was some nut lying in the bushes waiting for her.

The only good thing about it all, I told myself, was that if I was mad there were plenty of other people madder than me, and they were still running around on the loose.

It really was pretty tough trying to be normal in the village. Like I said, people were allergic to me because I was alive, but now – with the hints that I might be a coward and a deserter as well – they got really edgy. If they bumped into me and couldn't avoid me they didn't know how to react. You could almost see them thinking, do I say I'm sorry for all the hassle he's getting, or do I just tell him he's a shit?

Usually they just gave me a weak sort of smile and looked away. They were getting pretty paranoid, but then so was I. Even people who'd known me all my life, people whose houses I'd been allowed to treat as my own, started to shun me as if I might bring disaster into their homes. One bloke I knew, someone I'd knocked about with for years when we were at school, told me his parents actually warned him not to go within a mile of me in case I contaminated him. Of course they'd probably been the ones praying the hardest for the repose of my soul at the memorial service. Nice folk, you know.

Of course, while all this was going on, the press were still on at me. There'd be nothing about me for a week, and I'd think, great, they've finished at last. But then, somewhere, in a national or a local, someone would think up a new angle, and I'd be in the news again just so they could keep the ball rolling.

The reporters were still hanging around the village, sitting in their cars or lounging about trying to look inconspicuous. When I wouldn't go out to meet them and give them some titbit to write about, they started interviewing anything that moved. Little kids who hardly knew me were questioned and asked to give their opinion of me. Since they were too young to have any proper ideas of their own, they repeated what they'd heard their parents say, which sometimes sounded really scary coming from a child. Every girl within miles was grilled, and the things *they* were supposed to have said were something else, ending up in a story headlined RANDY

PHILIP AND THE GIRLS HE LEFT BEHIND. I learned I'd had affairs with twenty-five girls and broken all their goddamn hearts. Oh, I was a terrific lover too, which was good to know. I also learned that my sexual appetite was insatiable, that my willie refused to go down, that I could keep at it nonstop all night, and that girls were queuing up for my favours. It was a pity I never knew that myself.

All that crap made me laugh. It embarrassed the hell out of Mam though, even though she knew it was a pack of lies. And just for the record I may as well tell you that I'm no great shakes when it comes to sex. I mean, I like sex as much as the next bloke but I don't go round trying to sniff it out like it was depicted. And I've always been fussy who I go with. I like to be able to talk to the girl as well. Mind you, when word got around that I'd do it at the drop of a hat, the younger girls, those just starting to find out what it was all about and discovering that they liked it too, kept giving me those stupid looks; I think I could have lived up to my reputation if I'd wanted to. I'd be walking past a group of them, kids of twelve and thirteen, and they'd say things, pretending to be whispering but making sure I heard, that would make your hair stand on end. Make their Mums' hair stand on end anyway. To tell the truth I found it pretty disgusting but you couldn't blame the kids. They just wanted to experiment, and I'd been held up as something well worth experimenting with.

Then, for a while, there'd be nothing, and I'd start to relax again. But some more fantastic crap would be printed, like my steady girlfriend was sticking by me through thick and thin and wasn't about to abandon me in my hour of need, and that we were getting married in the autumn, which was news to me. I needn't have worried though. Another paper told me that Alison said I'd changed so much she couldn't put up with me, and that the planned wedding was off. Of course, they wrote the article in such a way as to make me sound a right bastard for changing.

It's really hard to describe what it was like in the house. I know I was going about a bit like a zombie. I just didn't want to get out of bed, and when I did I didn't know what to do with myself. Mam was so nervous she couldn't sit still for five minutes, and it didn't help with me under her feet all the time. Even Dad, who is pretty hard to shift, was jittery and edgy. He kept trying to be reasonable with the reporters though, always polite, always trying hard to keep his cool. Whenever any of them called me a hero, he'd say, 'I wish you wouldn't call our Phil that. He wasn't a hero. He was just trying to do the job he was sent to do.' I've often wondered if it was my Dad saying I wasn't a hero that started them off on their 'deserter' binge. I think Dad wonders about that too, and it worries the hell out of him. Lots of times I've wanted to tell him not to worry about it, since they'd have got round to making it up anyway. But we never talk about it, never talk about anything really. There never seems to be anything to say. Not for us, not now anyway.

That six weeks was the longest six weeks of my life. Much longer than the seven I'd been wandering about the bloody Falklands. But at last it came to an end, and it was time for me to return to the Scots Guards. I've never been so happy about anything. Everything was going to be all right now. Of course I couldn't go back without something in the paper to send me on my way. SOLDIER BACK FROM THE DEAD RETURNS TO HIS FIRST LOVE, I read. For a few lines, then, I was a good little boy again.

FIFTEEN

Mam has told me since that all I talked about during my leave was getting back to the Army. That strikes me as strange now. I suppose I felt I'd be safe back with the Guards. Thought, probably, that the Army would protect me from all the press hassle, and look after me. In a way all I had left *was* the Army, and they had seemed pleased enough to have me back. Mind you, there was no reason why I *shouldn't* go back. I'd turned up alive; been exonerated of any charges; and the reception I'd got by fellow soldiers at Ascension Island had been cordial to the Army's way of thinking. Yeah, sure he can come back, they said, the big brass anyway.

It didn't take me long to realise I wasn't exactly flavour of the month with the other soldiers, though.

I really did try to fit back in. I kept quiet as a mouse, and did pretty much as I was told. I joined the boxing team, and put everything I could into training, sweating my balls off in the boiler room to lose weight, even eating less to keep trim. I was getting pretty good at sparring too when, after a couple of weeks, the camp doctor put a stop to it, telling me it was too risky since I'd had memory losses within the last year. I know that was bullshit. I mean, sure I'd had memory losses but I was feeling fine, and getting better all the time. I'd bet my life that the rest of the team just didn't want me. I'd been getting a bit of verbal abuse from other guardsmen, but I didn't think they'd hate me that much. The daft thing was one day some pillock would tell me out of the corner of his mouth that I was a fucking disgrace to the Guards for pissing off on the Falklands, and the next day someone would be coming up to thank me for rescuing them off Tumbledown. I remember I used to wish they'd make up their sodding minds. It got so I didn't know what sort of answer to expect if I spoke to anyone, so I stopped talking and just kept myself to myself.

That didn't work either. Some of the more dim-witted guardsmen took it like I was stuck-up or something, too good for them. Between ourselves I probably was too good for those particular dumbos. There were about four of them in particular who kept needling me, 'What are you fucking doing in the Guards anyway, you shitting English coward?' and that sort of thing.

I was asleep. I thought I was having another nightmare until it dawned on me that some bastard really *was* using my goddamn face as a punchbag. He'd made quite a mess of me before I could start defending myself. It didn't altogether surprise me when I saw who it was. A right yobbo called Hinds. Thick. I mean *really* thick. I swear to you he was the nearest thing to an ape you ever did see, and the poor cunt thought he was the handsomest thing on two paws. Anyway, one of his mates pulled him off and dragged him out into the corridor to calm the sod down. I put it down to another one of life's little trials; well, I might have put it down to that, but I was damn sure I'd get Hinds for it sooner or later.

When I went to shave the next morning I got a bit of a shock: I looked almost as ugly as Hinds himself. There were three blue-black marks on my jaws and a deep enough cut over one eye. Unfortunately a corporal saw the mess I was in too, and told me to report to the Medical Officer.

The sick have to parade separately, and be inspected by a warrant officer, just in case any of them are skiving. He came up to me and stood in front of me. He didn't say anything for a while. Just stared at my face. Then he walked round me, and faced me again. 'Explain it,' he said. That's all.

I didn't say anything, just kept my eyes fixed away in the distance. I wouldn't want you to think I was being all noble and that sort of shit. It was nothing like that. I wanted to get my own back in my own time, and that was why I didn't answer.

'You tell me what happened or I'll charge *you*,' he said.

Well, sod that for a lark. I wasn't about to get myself charged just because some wanker didn't like my face the way it was. So I thought, bugger this, and told him so.

'Name?'

'Williams, sir.'

'Not yours. His.'

'Don't know, sir,' I said, which was a lie. 'Another company, sir,' I said, which was the truth.

'Well, find out his name.'

I told him I would and went off to the MO, thinking that the whole incident might be forgotten about.

The doctor prodded the bruises on my face and taped up the cut over my eye. 'You'll live,' he told me.

The warrant officer didn't forget about it though. He kept after me like he really wanted me to snitch. Just to get him off my back I told him it was Hinds. I felt pretty awful about telling. I thought that maybe Hinds would get banged up for a while, and I wouldn't wish that on anyone. I needn't have worried, though. He was put on a charge all right, but got off. They put it down to his drink problem, and anyway it was only me he'd attacked.

Probably because he got off so light, they had another go at me a couple of weeks later. Two of his mates; he didn't come himself, naturally. I was snoring my head off when they pounced and started belting me. They were clever enough not to mark my face this time, but they did a good job on my body. If I'd covered my head I'd have passed for a Paki no bother.

After that nobody bothered me for a while. They just ignored me, which suited me fine. In fact things were pretty normal for ten days or so. From staying in Chelsea

Barracks I'd got to know this civilian, a young bloke about my own age. I'd known him a little before I'd gone to the Falklands, and we met up again now. He didn't seem to care one way or the other if the stories about me were true. He never asked me about them, or about the war either for that matter. If he'd read the papers he never mentioned it. Sometimes we'd meet up and go for a drink and a chat, or have dinner in the Chelsea Kitchen on the Kings Road. Or, on a Saturday, we'd go to a soccer match at Stamford Bridge, behaving like ordinary people. Those might seem like trivial things, but they were really great to me. I began to think that everything was going to be okay.

They waited until I was asleep again. At least three of them this time. Right brave bastards. They tipped me out of bed and jumped on me. While I was still half asleep (and to be honest with a bit of a hangover) they tied me up with belts and ties. It was common knowledge that I smoked a bit of pot, like lots of others, when I could get it. So these shits must have been in the minority, because they kept yelling at me that I was nothing but a druggy scumbag, and that I was polluting the regiment.

'If you want drugs *we'll* fucking give them to you,' one of them said, and sat his great arse astride me, his knees on the inside of my elbows. The others forced my mouth open and rammed a load of tablets down my throat. I nearly choked, but they just kept piling more in. I don't know what the tablets were but they acted pretty damn fast and I could feel myself getting dizzy.

Everything got hazy like I was very, very drunk. I couldn't co-ordinate my movements at all. That suited them. They kicked the hell out of me, and easily dodged my efforts to defend myself. You can't do much when your hands are tied, and even less when your brain's tied up too.

For afters they dragged me down the corridor, taking it in turns to kick and punch me. Nobody bothered to help me. Nobody even came out to take a look what was happening. Maybe they knew it was me getting done in and weren't interested. Or maybe they were just like everyone else – didn't want to get involved.

Anyway, the three of them got tired of their sport at last, and just dumped me.

I suppose *someone* must have been a bit worried about the stick I was taking and reported it, since I started getting summoned to the Padre, and to Major Moody, the Families Officer.

The Padre was pretty nice. He never mentioned the bullying or anything, but he told me God watched over us all, which I guess was supposed to make me sleep easier. You could tell he was on very chummy terms with God: he knew a great deal about God's activities. Or he seemed to. I wanted to ask him what the hell God had been up to the nights I was having the shit kicked out of me, but I didn't. In a way *I* felt sorry for *him* – the Padre, I mean. He was only trying to do his job, and it's a pretty precarious one, you have to admit. Trying to get a load of yobbos like us to think about our souls, when all we really wanted was a beer and a screw and, in my case, a bit of pot, can't have been all that easy. I think he was feeling a bit redundant too. Padres were in great demand on the Falklands, working overtime, getting us into shape to meet our Maker just in case. But with that over, and poor old God not so popular now that we were unlikely to make His acquaintance for a while, they were back on the dole queue so to speak, and finding it tough to drum up business. Apart from the odd religious nut, the one who'd been Born Again, whatever that's supposed to mean, all he got was the ones who were *sent* to him, and we sort of resented that, treating him a bit like a holy quack.

Major Moody was okay too. He tried his best. The funny thing about him, he never once asked how *I* was, although I was the one who was supposed to be in need of his counselling. He was anxious to know how Mam was. And how Dad was. And how my little brother Gareth was. And how my sisters were. And he'd probably have asked after the goddamn cat if we'd had one. But me? Not on your nelly. I think the poor sod honestly believed I *had* to be all right. After all, I was in the great and good British Army, wasn't I?

Another thing was that he always said 'we' when he meant me. Like, 'How are we today?' Or, 'Getting on all right now, are we?' I know it was just his way of trying to be kind and put me at ease, but it sounded pretty bloody condescending really. Like he was doing me this big favour by lowering himself in the ranks, or maybe showing me he really understood what I was going through by pretending he was sharing it and was with me all the way, but knowing really he could piss off whenever he liked and have a gin and tonic and a good laugh with his fellow officers while I probably went back to have the crap kicked out of me again.

The trouble was, of course, that neither the Padre or the Major wanted to admit that I was getting bullied. If they did that then they'd have to instigate an investigation, and once they started Christ knows where it would end. Besides, everyone said such things didn't happen in the Scots Guards, and they weren't about to admit that it did just because of me, especially since I never made any formal complaint unless I was pushed to it.

SIXTEEN

Just before Christmas I was sent back on public duty. I did the Tower of London a couple of times. The first time I was standing there like a dummy thinking to myself, Fuck it, I don't have to put up with all this crap I'm getting about being a newspaper hero, and being a frigging deserter. So I walked off, sat down behind a wall and had a cigarette. It didn't seem that I was away that long but I heard later it was about half an hour. Needless to say the guard patrol went haywire searching for me. Someone told me later they thought I might have jumped off the bloody tower. The shit would really have hit the fan then. I got a right bollocking for that, but they didn't lock me up. By that time they were scared to lay a finger on me in case the press got a whisper of it.

My second stint at the Tower was on Christmas Day, when suddenly I got this awful pain in my stomach right in the middle of the Ceremony of the Keys. I know the rest of them thought I was arsing around, trying to make a mockery of the ceremony. The pain was so bad that I passed out, and they had to believe it when they had to carry me off to the guardroom. In the guardroom I vomited my guts out, and just kept on puking even though there was nothing left inside me. When the ceremony was over I was loaded up with the others and taken back to Chelsea. The pain was still crucifying me, but as I was supposed to start a couple of weeks of leave the next day, I tried to play it down and pretend everything was okay.

I was just collecting my wages when the sergeant let a roar out of him for me to come over to where he was. He was furious, ranting on about how I'd been 'out of order' getting sick on duty, as if I'd planned it, and going on again about my sneaking off for that fag, making both incidents sound like skiving. As if to prove to himself that the pain was all in my imagination he thumped me as hard as he could in the stomach, and told me to get out of his fucking sight before he changed his mind and had me locked up for negligence.

I can tell you I was glad to get out of the barracks, even if I had to walk out of there alone while all the others were leaving in twos and threes, laughing and enjoying themselves. Old Lancaster seemed like paradise, so I must really have been in a state. I even set off for the station, but the pain in my stomach got so bad I decided to stay in the Union Jack club for the night. I didn't eat or drink anything, just hauled myself into bed and lay there all curled up.

During the night the pain got worse. It got so bad that I really thought I was going to die. Someone called a doctor. He poked me a bit and asked if I'd had my appendix out even though the scar was staring him in the face. He decided that it wasn't anything serious, but left me a couple of Aspros just in case – in case of what, I don't know. Maybe it was because they were the only thing he had on him that was handy. I remember he was all dressed up, and he'd emptied a bucket full of aftershave over himself. His hair was all slicked down with Brylcreem, and I kept thinking he looked like one of those gangsters in old black-and-white films. I wondered if I'd interrupted some secret date he had with his moll, a moll his wife didn't know about, of course. One thing I could tell. I could tell he was peeved at being called out. Anyway, the pain had eased off again so I didn't mind.

The next morning I got the train to Lancaster.

The closer I got to home the more scared I got. I was really looking forward to seeing my Mam and Dad but I was frightened about what might be waiting for me in Halton. I had visions of pressmen ganging up on me again, and of the locals stoning me. I suppose I must have known this was going to happen because I hadn't even told my parents I was getting leave, just in case I couldn't face the village. And a good job I never did tell them because when I got to Lancaster I couldn't face going any further. I simply, physically, could not make myself get on that bus.

I stayed with a friend in Lancaster, and ignored Christmas. I couldn't ignore my stomach since the pain was back again twice as bad as before. The funny thing was my parents weren't even at home. They'd gone off on holiday to get some sun.

Even in a place the size of Lancaster, though, I felt uneasy. I had this thing about people looking at me, even if they weren't. And anyone who did must have thought I was pig ignorant since I'd just glare back at them.

The worst thing was that I knew now I was lost. I didn't belong to either military or civilian life. I wanted to get away from both of them. About two days before I was due to return to Chelsea it dawned on me: I was, in the strangest way, a fugitive. I wanted to go home but was afraid to. I wanted to go back to the barracks but was afraid of doing that, too.

I know it was a crazy thing to do, but the way my mind was working at the time it seemed very sensible. Okay, I thought, if you are a fugitive, be one. I purposely missed the train back to London. I went AWOL.

At first it was pretty exciting being on the run, as I thought of it. I even played daft games with myself, diving into shop doorways and waiting there to see if I was being followed. Or if I was going somewhere I'd take a really roundabout way, crossing and recrossing the road, even jumping on a bus and jumping off again between stops. But, you know — and this is the oddest thing ever — I felt quite bad about it. Somewhere inside me, I think, there was some dumb sense of duty. Anyway, whatever the reason, I phoned up the Company Commander.

He was quite nice to begin with, very considerate and fatherly. He wanted me to give myself up. 'I urge you to give yourself up.' That's exactly what he said.

'Shit no,' I told him.

'If there's a problem we can sort it out, I'm sure.'

'Oh sure.'

'*Is* there a problem?'

'Of course there's a fucking problem,' I said, and heard him gasp a bit. Well, you'd think he'd *know* there was a problem, wouldn't you?

'Why not give yourself up and come and talk to me about it?' he said, reasonably enough.

I didn't feel like being reasonable. 'I'm not giving myself up,' I replied. 'And I'm frigging well fed up with being bullied and having the shit kicked out of me and fucking pills shoved down my throat and nothing done about it.'

Instantly his attitude changed and he started telling me not to be making such wild accusations that, as he said, 'had no foundation in reality'.

'You think I'm making it up?'

'No. No, I wouldn't say that exactly.'

'Well, what would you bloody well say exactly?'

'Your imagination, perhaps. You've been through – '

I slammed the phone down. Maybe I shouldn't have. Maybe I should have given him the chance to finish what he was saying. Maybe a lot of things.

A bit of panic set in as soon as I got out of the phonebox. I started imagining stupid things. Like them tracing the call and finding out where I was. Like the whole Army being mobilised to descend on Lancaster to arrest me. Seriously.

I decided I'd better get out. I went to Morecambe to stay with my Auntie Iris. You'd like my Auntie Iris. She's a right good sort, and as honest and straight with you as the day is long. My family can't stand her, though. Always bitching about how she drinks too much. Not that she thinks a hell of a lot of my family. 'Lot of bloody jumped-up snobs,' she calls them. 'Just 'cause they've got a posh car they think they're better class,' she says. Then she'll keel over laughing because she knows she's right, and she knows, too, that everyone can see through the crappy airs my family tries to put on.

We got on like a house on fire. She'd heard all about me and the Falklands and didn't give a damn one way or the other. 'I don't want to hear nowt about it,' she told me. 'You are family and that's all that matters to me. Best of the lot, you are, Phil. That's why they're picking on you. The trouble with that lot in Halton is they're afraid to be honest even with themselves. To hell with them.'

'That's it, Auntie.'

'Let's have a bit of a tipple, lad.'

'Good idea, Auntie. Fuck 'em all.'

Auntie hooted at that.

SEVENTEEN

All the time I was with Auntie Iris, I kept trying to get my parents on the phone. I knew they'd be worried. I wanted them to know where I was, and that I was all right. I thought they'd understand why I needed to take off for a bit. Sure I expected some flack, but not the amount I got. They went berserk with me for going AWOL, not even wanting to know why.

'We've been frantic,' Mam said.

'I'm okay, Mam. I'm with Auntie Iris.'

'You've ruined our holiday.'

'Sorry, Mam,' I told her, although I wasn't really. They'd had their holiday before they found out I was AWOL so I don't see how I could have ruined it.

'We've been on to the Scots Guards.'

'Shit. What did you do that for?'

'Everything's all right. They're not going to lock you up or anything. They've promised to be very fair with you.'

'Bullshit. Thanks a lot, Mam. You've really landed me in it now.'

'Don't be stupid. They don't know where you are.'

'You didn't tell them?'

'We didn't know, did we?'

'Oh. Sorry, Mam. I just need a bit of time to think. I'll go back soon enough, I promise.'

'You're to go back now,' Mam told me.

'Not yet.'

'You're just making things worse.'

'Not yet.'

'Yes. Now. Straight away,' Mam insisted.

I could feel myself getting all worked up into a sweat. I knew, I don't know how, but I did, that my parents were going to tell the Army where I was, and Mam was pressing me to give myself up so that they wouldn't have to. Or so that I wouldn't find out that it was them who shopped me. I remember very clearly saying to Mam, 'You won't say where I am, will you, Mam?' and Mam saying, 'Of course not.'

Fifteen minutes later the police were at Auntie Iris's door. Auntie Iris saw them coming and told me to get into the kitchen quick, while she went to the door. Poor Auntie Iris, she really tried her best to bluff them, but they just kept saying, 'We know he's here.' I thought about doing a bunk through the back garden, but they'd thought of that: another one of them was standing there gawping up at the house.

'Nothing's going to happen to him,' the policeman was telling Auntie.

'Huh,' I heard Auntie grunt, and that made me smile.

'You have my word on that,' the policeman told her.

To be fair, they were okay with Auntie Iris. They didn't threaten her or bully her. Maybe that was their tactic. If it was, it worked. Auntie Iris believed everything would be okay if I gave up.

'It's no use, Phil,' she said, coming into the kitchen. 'They know you're here. Better go with them, lad.' Then she cuddled me really tight. She was crying hard too.

I was surprised that the pig waiting for me was a civilian policeman. I suppose I'd been expecting military police with civilian backup. I said, 'What's this got to do with you bastards?'

'Now, laddie, don't be offensive.'

'Piss off.'

'Just come along or we'll have to handcuff you.'

'Just fucking try it.'

'We're just going to hold you till the Guards come and deal with it.'

'It' was me, by the way.

In one way the police cell was fine. I was alone. Nobody interfering. Time, I thought, to think. But I couldn't think. I couldn't get my mind to focus on anything. I'd start off all right but then it would wander off, and start shaping up things of its own. I'd think I was sitting there quietly, minding my own business, and then I'd realise I was hammering on the door, shouting and screaming and swearing. And I could *see* myself doing this. It was like there were two of me there, one watching the other. What I didn't know until the quack told me later, was that I'd had a nervous breakdown, whatever that is.

Sometime during the night a policewoman opened the slot in the door to say my parents wanted to visit me. I just stared at her. I was thinking what shit that was. First they shop me, get me into this fucking mess and then they want to come and gape at me. 'Fuck them,' I said.

'You don't have to see them,' the policewoman told me, as if she understood what was happening to me. 'As a detainee you have the right to refuse.'

'You bet I fucking refuse.'

After that I couldn't sleep although I tried to. I was exhausted, actually shaking with tiredness. Everything was piling up on top of me again. I kept thinking the press would make another meal out of this. And the shit would be kicked out of me when they got me back to Chelsea. And my own parents had landed me in it. Christ, couldn't anyone leave me alone to work out my own problems? Everyone was treating me like a right moron. Everyone was doing things to me and telling me it was for my own good. What the hell did they know? How could they know what was good for me? All I'd ever wanted was to be a soldier. I'd been a soldier. I'd fought as best I could. I'd rescued a few people. Then I'd got lost. Why was I now going through all this shit just because of that?

They brought me breakfast. I told them to piss off with their bloody breakfast which was a stupid thing to do. I was starving and the food didn't look at all bad. I felt it was as if bringing me breakfast was another perverted favour, and if I accepted it I'd find myself in more trouble.

Later two Scots Guards in plain clothes collected me and took me to Morecambe station. We had a while to wait, and they offered me food and drink. I didn't make the same mistake this time, and had a couple of pasties and a beer. They were okay, those two. All the way up on the train we chatted. One of them said, 'It's always poor sods like you who get done,' and I think he meant it, but maybe they'd been trained to say things like that to keep poor sods like me quiet.

A Land Rover picked us up at Euston. I was now nervous as hell, wondering what was going to happen, and thinking the worst, of course. My escorts weren't so chatty now, either. The closer we got to Chelsea the less human they seemed to get.

'Ah, Williams,' the Regimental Sergeant Major said, looking up from a pile of papers, eyeing me and looking away again like I might hypnotise him or give him the evil eye. 'Nothing to worry about,' he went on. 'Tomorrow it's the hospital for you. Treatment. For now, though, guardroom. Can't have you taking off again, can we?'

So off they trundled me to the guardroom. The Guard Sergeant was a right dickhead, built like a bull. They pick them special, I think; lack of brains is essential. And they're not allowed to talk: they have to shout or keep quiet. This one wasn't about to keep quiet. He kept ranting away, telling me what a shitting sorry sight I was, what sort of an excuse did I think I was for a Scots Guardsman, who did I think I was putting the Army to such trouble – that sort of shit. I was glad when he slammed the door and locked it.

I was only there for half an hour when he was back again with my regulation food, making me stand to attention before I accepted it, giving me a load more crap about how if he had his way I wouldn't be fed at all.

He was still ranting when the RSM walked in. That shut him up pretty quick. The RSM went bananas. 'What's that man doing locked up?' he wanted to know.

Fuckface tried to answer but the RSM wasn't about to listen. 'That man is not to be treated as a prisoner. Not locked up, understand? Free access to television, understand?'

The Guard Sergeant understood.

I couldn't resist it. I walked out of my cell and as I passed him I gave the Guard Sergeant a wink. I thought he was going to explode. I had this vision of the blood rising up his face to the top of his head and blowing his stupid cap off. That made me smile at him, too. I toddled off to the corner and poured myself a mug of tea from the urn, and then, very casually, exaggerating it, sauntered into the TV room and sat down.

'Out,' the Guard Sergeant said to me early next morning.

I walked, taking my time, out of my cell.

'Proper little film star we have here, haven't we?'

'What's that supposed to mean?' I asked.

'Been sounding off about our mates to the newspapers, haven't we?'

'Have I shit.'

'Papers don't lie.'

'Like fuck they don't.'

I learned later that the *Telegraph* had reported that the Army were investigating allegations I was supposed to have made about being taunted by fellow soldiers over my missing weeks on the Falklands. They also mentioned that I'd been arrested for going absent without leave.

It was only when I was in the transport that I was told I was being taken to Woolwich hospital. You might think that this put the wind up me. It didn't. It was a terrific bloody relief. I'd been in Woolwich before when my leg was smashed up, so I knew what it was like.

The trip didn't take long. I was given a small bag with pyjamas, shaving gear, toothbrush and toothpaste, and left at Ward Reception. It was really weird the way my escort did that, just left me standing there and marched off without a word. I expect they were glad to get rid of me, and hand the responsibility over to someone else.

I had to sign a couple of admittance forms so that the Guards wouldn't be blamed for committing me, and was told the doors were never locked. When I didn't react, it was repeated like it was important for me to understand. 'The doors are *never* locked here.'

'Fancy that,' I think I said, or something equally daft.

'We just want you to take it easy.'

'That's fine by me.'

'And smoking *is* permitted.'

'Smoking what?'
'Tobacco, of course.'
'Oh.'
Anyway, when the formalities were over I was finally put on Ward 5, the one they reserve for the mental patients, although that includes alcoholics as well.

It was like being in heaven.

EIGHTEEN

There were a few things going on at home too, even without me being there. Needless to say the press had found out about my being AWOL and had besieged my home. But my parents had got wise to them by now and didn't say anything. They were getting pretty fed up with the whole thing anyway, wanting to get back to their own lives, for which you can't blame them. What they really wanted, of course, was for the Army to sort something out for me. And it was probably this that made Dad go down south to London and see Lieutenant-Colonel Mike Scott. I'd like to have been there. If I'd been at home I'd have told Dad not to waste his time, but I wasn't and Dad had to find out for himself. Of course they ran rings about him. My Dad never has much to say and isn't the greatest with words. Mind you, he didn't have to be. The Lieutenant-Colonel wasn't about to let him say much. He started off by treating Dad as a friend, agreeing it was such a shame that I'd got myself in such a pickle, but making it clear he was sure I was exaggerating the bullying — such things didn't happen in the Guards, not the Scots Guards anyway.

When that didn't seem to work he tried to impress Dad, telling him the Duke of Kent had been sitting in the very chair he was now sitting in. Dad didn't give a toss about the Duke of Kent. Probably didn't even know who he was, apart from the fact that he didn't drive a lorry like himself.

'The best thing, for the present,' the Lieutenant-Colonel said, 'is to keep things as — well, as quiet as possible. Keep the wretched press out of it, you understand.'

Dad understood.

'We have, of course, launched our own investigation into your son's allegations. We have, in fact, reprimanded two soldiers from the regiment.'

'So you admit he was bullied?' Dad asked.

'Well, no. Not precisely. There were some irregularities which have now been dealt with. To be truthful, Mr Williams, we don't really think your son was cut out to be a soldier.'

What he meant by that, I suppose, was that the Guard's hope that getting me back into the regiment to smooth over what they always referred to as 'the Falklands incident' had failed.

'Meanwhile we are doing everything possible for his welfare. He is in excellent hands in Woolwich, you know.'

And that's as much as Dad got out of them, although

he was promised that the Guards only had my wellbeing at heart and that I would certainly be their 'concern' when I was released from Woolwich. It just shows you how convincing they can be: Dad believed all that bullshit. And I don't blame him. It would take someone a lot cleverer than Dad to see through their crap. And in a way you can't blame the Guards for trying to hoodwink him. They were getting flack from other sources. There was a lieutenant called Lawrence who was stirring up a bit of shit of his own, and he had quite some clout which made them very nervous: you can't just dismiss what an officer says the way you can someone from the ranks.

Anyway, Dad came home and told Mam what had been said, and Mam said something like, 'Oh good', thinking everything would be fine from now on. She wrote to me in Woolwich and told me about it. I didn't want to hear. I'd already *heard* all that. I knew all about Lieutenant-Colonel Mike Scott. He was the one who'd made the press release saying that I 'did well to survive as well as he did with his limited experience. I am satisfied that he did all that he could to get back to his unit as quickly as possible'.

A lot of fucking good that had done me.

One really nice thing happened, though. One of the soldiers I'd rescued wrote to my parents. It really touched me that he went to the trouble to sit down and actually write, especially since I couldn't remember who he was. He told them how I'd got him off Tumbledown after

he'd been shot in the head, and how I'd cheered him up.
I don't remember cheering anyone up. But he sure as hell
cheered me up. Made me feel really chuffed, whoever he
was.

NINETEEN

So there I was, all tucked up in Woolwich hospital with my nervous breakdown. Both of us neatly out of the way. I must admit that I found it all great fun, but maybe that was because I *was* slightly off the rails.

The treatment was the daftest thing I'd ever come across. We had to see the shrink once a week, and the rest of the time was spent on occupational therapy. You want to know what that is? Well, occupational therapy is doing woodwork or making toys. I did a lot of it. I shoved more fucking wool up the arses of more fucking fluffy rabbits than there were sheep on the Falklands, and there had been millions of them.

In the evenings we all sat like zombies round the telly, gawping at it. We could never switch from one channel to the other because if someone tried that a fight would certainly break out. So we just sat there watching whatever happened to turn up.

The visits to the shrink, Major Cantly, seemed pretty useless too.

'And how are we feeling?'

'Oh, we're feeling fine.'

'Good, good. We'll soon have to be thinking what's to become of you on your release, won't we?'

'Indeed we will.'

'And have you thought about it?'

'Oh yes.'

'Excellent,' he'd say, and wait for me to tell him what I'd been thinking.

I always wanted to say something really stupid like, 'Well, I thought I might join Napoleon on his march into Moscow,' but then I thought maybe they'd believe I really was crazy and lock me away for good, and throw away the key, so I'd say, 'Well, I haven't really decided yet.'

'Of course not. No. Well, we have time to think about it, don't we?'

'Yes.'

'But not, I think, the Army for you, eh?'

That was his way of telling me that the Army had decided they didn't want me, which was fair enough. I didn't want them so that made us even, but I wasn't about to let on about *that* just yet.

There was this really strange attitude on my ward in Woolwich. The nurses were nice and all, and they'd been told, I suppose, that it was bad for us to be allowed to show emotion. We were soldiers and even if we were diagnosed as nuts we still were supposed to be brave and tough and keep our feelings under control. A couple of the lads there cried a lot and they would get bollocked for that: crying was forbidden.

We had this little Gurkha on our ward. Christ, he was only about four foot shit but he looked as though he'd eat any two of us for breakfast. He didn't like the rest of us much. At first I thought he was just a cracked racist, but I soon found out it wasn't that. He'd been brainwashed into believing that the Gurkhas were superior to any other regiment, just like I'd had it drilled into me that the Scots Guards were top of the heap. To tell the truth I felt quite sorry for him. He couldn't hardly speak English, so we never really knew his name. We used to call him Fred or Simba, not that he answered us. He was going through a pretty bad time. I think something strange must have happened to him on the Falklands because he kept having nightmares. I tried to get him to tell me about it in his own language. I thought talking about it to me might help him a bit. But he wouldn't. Every so often he'd pack up all his kit and leave it by the door of the ward, ready to make a break for it during the night, but the poor sod was so full of pills and tranks that the night staff had no bother keeping him in bed. Then they'd put all his gear away for him, and the next morning he'd have forgotten he'd been planning to take off. Until the next time the fit got him; then we'd go through all the whole pantomime again.

Things got a bit better when I met another patient called Karen. She was a major's daughter and was in for slimmer's disease. I only got to talk to her in the evenings since she went to college during the day. We got on pretty well. They let us out sometimes and off we'd go for a beer or to the cinema. We were just friends, but only because we were both in hospital. She wasn't my type, and I know I wasn't hers. We'd never have even spoken to each other on the outside, I don't think.

Not that it was always as nice as it sounds. A couple of military police came to see me, saying they were there to take a statement about the alleged bullying. But before they got round to that they searched all my belongings, hoping they'd find some hash. They didn't.

'Tough,' I told them.

'Why tough?'

'Didn't find nowt, did you?'

'Don't need to, laddie. We know you smoke the crap, that's enough.'

'You'll have a job proving it.'

'Don't *have* to, laddie. Nobody believes the shit you've been giving about your mates anyway.'

'Some fucking mates.'

'The best *you'll* ever have.'

'You want a statement or not?'

'Say what you like.'

'You going to take it down?'

'Sure we'll take it down. Every fucking word.'

They did too, but I could see they didn't believe anything I said. I don't even know if they wrote down *what* I said. I didn't care either. Even if *they* reported what I said it would be twisted around at the other end, just to keep the reputation of the Scots Guards intact, of course.

And Dad phoned me to say my Nana had died. I was really shattered by that. She'd been ill for a couple of weeks and nobody'd told me.

'Why didn't you tell me she was sick?'

Dad didn't answer.

'You don't give a shit about me, do you?'

Dad didn't answer that either.

'It would have suited you all better if I *had* bloody died on the Falklands, wouldn't it?'

I was really pissed off. I felt like that I'd been shut away so no one would have to be bothered remembering me: not the Army, not my family, nobody. Like they were saying, 'We won't bother telling Phil. He's mad anyway, so he won't want to know.'

Well, like it or not, I was going to get to that funeral. And the staff were pretty good about it. They arranged a one-week leave for me, and I should have been a bit more grateful.

'You can have one week's leave.'

'Big deal.'

'And mind you come back on time. No more scarpering from you.'

'I'll be back, don't worry.'

'Seriously. Don't do anything stupid. We're sorting out your release, and you'll only bugger things up.'

It was news to me that they were sorting out my release. I found it hard to believe that I'd been there nearly six months. I wasn't feeling any different but I must have been showing something. Maybe it was the way I stuffed the bunnies. Great thing, that occupational therapy, when you apply yourself.

In the end I was sorry I went. It wasn't the best way to reintroduce myself to the big wide world. Everyone pushing around trying to look sad, and all the time staring at me to see what a lunatic looked like. Then I'd look them in the eye and they'd smile their best smile at me, then remember it was a funeral and that they weren't supposed to be smiling, and they'd glare at me like they were blaming me for that too.

And the ceremony was awful. A real quickie like the minister had other things to do and was annoyed at Nana for interrupting his schedule. He gabbled a few words about Nana, but what he said could have applied to anyone. I suppose he used the same old crap he spouts out for everyone. Saves him thinking. And another thing: the church was pretty empty, and those friends of Nana who had come were all as old as herself. You could *see* them wondering if they'd be next, and you could tell they were worrying if this was all the send off they'd be given.

As I was leaving the church I heard these two old ones whispering to themselves. 'That's him,' one said.

'*That's* him?'

'That's him.'

I needn't say who 'him' was, need I?

'He got a better funeral. And he's not even dead.'

'That's what I mean.'

That cheered me up. I really did have to laugh. It kind of summed everything up. Nobody wanted me alive. I'd have been the greatest thing since sliced bread if I'd died. Alive I was nothing but a fucking nuisance. Really made me feel good, that did.

I didn't take the full leave and went back to Woolwich after only a few days. I'd started getting these terrible pains again in my stomach, and had a right belter the night before I went back. Doubled me up. They all thought I was about to have a fit or something, and started getting out of the room as fast as they could. When the pain eased I wanted to put on a terrific act, put soap in my mouth so I'd froth and go chasing down the street, screaming. Really give them something to talk about. But I chickened out. What was the point? I'd be the only one laughing, and a joke isn't really a joke unless you share it.

They were surprised at Woolwich when I showed up early. Someone, without thinking, asked if I hadn't enjoyed myself.

'Smashing,' I said. 'Nothing like a good funeral for a laugh.'

'Oh, sorry.'

'That's okay. I missed my own so I go to anyone's now.'

Anyway, the ward doctor examined me, and gave me some tablets which didn't work. I kept telling them they weren't working, but was told, they will, they will. They didn't, so after three days they arranged for a scan.

'Well,' the ward doctor told me later. 'You've got two ulcers.' He sounded a bit like he was telling some woman she'd had a bouncing boy, smiling away to himself at his discovery.

'Great,' I said. 'That's all I need.'

It wasn't all I needed apparently. I had to have a different medication and a new ward, this one for people with internal problems: ulcers, kidney stones and the like.

Because of the pain they used to give me some stuff to help me sleep. I wish I knew the name of it. It was better than any hash I've ever had, at least while I was falling asleep. The trouble was that once I actually got to sleep I'd have these awful nightmares. I only remember one of them. In it old Pete, my dead companion, and the goose I blew up got muddled together, and I ended up tearing bits off Pete and shoving them into my mouth. I had it quite often and each time woke up screaming my bloody head off. The shrink heard about it and asked me what I was dreaming about, but I didn't dare tell him in case he decided I'd been into a bit of cannibalism during my travels, and Christ knows what they'd have done to me then. I just said I didn't know. I also said I didn't know when he asked me what I thought I would do on my release from hospital. He nodded at that. 'We've been trying very hard to decide your future in the Army.'

I know he was dying for me to say that I didn't *want* any future in the fucking Army. That would have let them off the hook. But I just nodded the way he'd done.

'Would you consider looking for an alternative?'

You bet your bloody life I would, I thought. But I just said, 'Maybe. Depends.'

'Of course. That's very reasonable,' he told me, a bit surprised as if he'd been expecting me to be unreasonable. And you know what he said then? Jesus! He said, 'However, perhaps you should. We feel, you see, that you might have lost your military mind.'

How about that for a whopping beauty? Lost my fucking military mind. I felt like jumping up and down and cheering. If I had really lost my military mind I'd be the happiest sod in the whole wide world.

Another funny thing about Woolwich. The domestic staff did more to rehabilitate us than all the quacks put together. They really went out of their way to be cheerful and to cheer us up too. There was one Scottish girl called Morag who was a right gas. She made the coffee and tea and stuff like that. She never came into the ward without this big grin on her face, and if we tried to take the piss out of her she'd give us back every bit as good as she got. It was great to have someone treating us as if we were fairly normal. She arranged the flowers that friends and relatives sent to some of the patients; she really took great care over doing that, making them look as pretty as possible. And sometimes she'd stick one between her teeth and do this daft dance just to make us laugh. We all decided if they shot the doctors and gave us half a dozen Morags we'd be out of that place within days. I wonder if she's still there?

One evening in the summer of 1983 I was pottering about the ward, getting ready for bed. A nurse came up to me and said, 'You better get your things together. You're leaving us first thing in the morning.'

'Where to?'

'I don't know. I was just told to tell you that you're leaving here.'

After that, of course, I couldn't sleep, even with their lousy pills. I was so worried. What were the bastards going to do with me now? I kept thinking that maybe I'd gone too far somewhere and this time they were really going to send me to a funny farm. I kept seeing myself in some cell, in a straitjacket, with nobody knowing where I was, or caring either.

Then the night nurse came on duty, one of the ones I got on well with. She came over to me, smiling. 'I bet *you're* a happy young man tonight.'

'How's that?'

'Getting your discharge tomorrow?'

'Discharge?'

'That's right. This time tomorrow you'll be a civilian.'

After that I couldn't sleep at all. I was so excited. Jesus, at last I was getting out of all this shit. I could go off and be by myself and no one would be interested in me any more. What a sucker I was.

TWENTY

All the way from Woolwich to Chelsea I kept urging in my mind the transport to go quicker. I couldn't wait to be free again. I also kept wondering if this was another military wind-up; that the news of the discharge was just their way of keeping me calm for the journey.

Once back in the barracks I was told to go and collect whatever possessions I had there. That didn't take long as I'd got practically nothing, and what I did have was hardly worth collecting. Then I was told to go and get the pay that was due to me. That didn't take long either. Two hundred quid. They had it all ready for me. The last order I got was to report to the commanding officer, Lieutenant-Colonel Mike Scott, the guy who'd bamboozled Dad.

I had to march in, but I didn't mind as it would be the last time I'd march anywhere. The Lieutenant-Colonel started giving me his old bullshit about how it was such a pity I hadn't made it as a guardsman, but overall I'd got a good discharge report, which would certainly help me, wouldn't it?

I said, 'Yes sir. Thank you, sir.' Three fucking bags full, sir.

'Not everyone makes it, you know,' he told me. That was my consolation prize. 'Just sign there.'

I signed my discharge. I signed it carefully so that there'd be no mistake. And put a nice round fullstop at the end.

'Good,' the Lieutenant-Colonel said. 'Oh, and this is yours, of course.'

Of course. He handed me my Falklands Campaign Medal. It was attached to a piece of card.

THIS IS TO CERTIFY THAT GUARDSMAN PHILIP WILLIAMS TOOK PART IN THE BATTLE FOR MOUNT TUMBLEDOWN. WELL DONE. BEST WISHES. YOUR COMMANDING OFFICER M. SCOTT.

The Lieutenant-Colonel beamed at me. 'Good luck to you now,' he said. And that was that. I walked out of Chelsea Barracks. I had the stupidest smile on my face. It was like my goddamn birthday. I was nineteen.

BOOK THREE

TWENTY-ONE

You'll probably think I was a right wanker when I tell you what I did first. And I won't argue, since you're probably right. I went to Brixton to find some hash. I just wanted a bit to calm me down. It does that to me. And it wasn't hard to find as it was on sale all over the place. These guys looked upset if you didn't buy. There was this very jolly-looking Rastafarian bloke, smiling away, so I bought a bit off him just so that he wouldn't be offended. I told him I was celebrating getting out of the Army.

'Hey man, that's great,' he told me.

'Better than great. Bloody marvellous.'

'You got a place to stay? Can get you a nice room in a squat if you like,' he said.

'I'm not staying. Not in stinking London anyway. Besides, I've got plans.'

'Wow-eeee,' he said. 'The man's got plans.'

I caught the tube to Euston, bought a few beers, and got on the train to Lancaster. I was really excited about going home. Things would be great now that I was a civilian again.

I stayed the first night at my parents' house. They didn't say a lot to me once they'd said, 'How are you,' and I'd said, 'Okay.' I could tell they were uneasy having me there, but I didn't know why. I still don't, but I suppose it was because they thought I'd bring nothing but trouble with me again. The next morning, though, they had plenty to say.

'Why you ever left the Army I'll never understand,' Dad said.

I couldn't think of an answer to that. Well I could, but I didn't want to start the day off with a row.

'You'll have to get a job, you know. You can't expect to live at home doing nothing,' was Mam's contribution.

'I'll get a job,' I said. 'Give me a break, Mam.'

'You should be out now looking for one. They're crying out for ex-servicemen.'

'Let them sodding cry.'

'The longer you leave it the harder it'll be to get a good job, and you can't live in the world today without a job.'

'I told you – I'll get a job. Shit, I only got out yesterday.'

'Don't say that word. I know you, Phil Williams. You'll let the days and weeks go by just mooching around and never make up your mind to do anything.'

'Oh, fuck this,' I said and walked out.

I went to stay with my sister Angie. We get on okay mostly. At least she tried to understand what I was going through. I know she really couldn't, but she tried.

'Want to talk about it, Phil?'

'No.'

'Okay, suit yourself. I know what's the matter with you anyway.'

'Oh yeah?'

'Sure.'

'What then?'

She put on this great big grin. 'You're mad as a fucking hatter.'

A couple of weeks later Mam rang Angie to say the press had been round again. They wanted to know what sort of discharge I'd got. Was it true I'd been court-martialled and kicked out? Or had I just walked out and gone AWOL again? Was it true I was back with Alison again and that we were going to get married? And the bullying I'd gone through, had I really been crippled?

I was gone from Halton that night.

I went to Morecambe. I liked Morecambe, even if it is a run-down, bankrupt holiday resort next to a nuclear power plant. I'd been safe there once for a while with Auntie Iris, and I suppose I thought I might be safe there again. I found myself a little flat, not far from Auntie Iris's home. It was great. Nobody hassling me or telling me I should do this or that. And Iris and my cousin Carol were always there if I needed them or their shoulders to cry on.

One day an old mate of mine we called Plank came round. 'I'm going to Tenby for the weekend. Want to come?'

'Where's bloody Tenby?'

'Wales.'

'Wales!'

'Yeah, Wales.'

'Okay. Why not? They won't miss me at the office.'

'Your secretary can run things, can she?'

'Right on.'

We didn't have much money between us but we decided to splurge and get the coach to Birmingham to give ourselves a head start. That took about four hours but we enjoyed every minute of it. We were just like a couple of kids on a school outing or something; everything seemed funny, and we laughed our heads off all the way, usually at nothing. In Birmingham we caught a local bus to the edge of town, and another one to the other side of the Avon. Then we started hitch-hiking.

Cars and lorries just whizzed past us. Nobody was going to give us scruffy-looking pair a lift, it seemed. I bet half of them were wondering what sort of disease we'd leave in their back seats, and the other half weren't taking a chance on being mugged. But even that seemed funny, and we had a good laugh as we marched along.

'Fuck this walking,' he kept saying.

'Good for you,' I told him.

'Give us a piggy-back.'

'Like hell.'

'Go on.'

'Okay.'

So Plank took both the backpacks and hopped on to my back, and you should have seen the looks the pair of us got as I trotted along the edge of the road. I swear to God cars were swerving all over the place.

By the time it was dark we still hadn't got a lift so we decided to find somewhere to sleep, somewhere nice and secluded so we could put up our tent. We cut away from the road and after a while came to this high, chainlink fence. We could just make out some trees inside, and decided that would suit us nicely. We clambered over the fence, and pitched our tent under the trees. In no time we fell asleep.

The next thing Plank was shaking me. 'There's someone outside,' he whispered.

'Sod them.' I was knackered.

'Shit Jesus,' was the next thing he said, and started scrambling about the tent as if he'd gone berserk.

Not that I blame him. When I looked out I thought I was going mad too. There were five or six Indian buffalo staring me in the eye. We'd spent the night in some bloody safari park. I can tell you we were out of there and over that fence without touching it before those fucking buffalo had a chance to blink again.

Anyway, without any other major adventures we reached Tenby. I was glad I'd agreed to come. The sea was so blue and the sand such a white bright, nothing like the murky shore in the Falklands or Morecambe Bay with all its stinking pollution. Jesus, it was fabulous. We acted like kids again because that was the way we felt. Really young. All we did was get sunburned and laugh a lot. No drink, no pot, no girls. Just laugh and laugh at nothing except the fact that we were happy. It was the best holiday I'd ever had. It still is, really.

'What you going to do, Phil?'

'Don't know.'

'No ideas?'

'None.'

'Well, shit, don't worry about it. Something will turn up.'

'Sure.'

'Course it will,' Plank said. 'Always does, doesn't it?'

'You guarantee that?'

'Sure I guarantee it. Okay? So cheer up.'

'Shit, I *was* cheerful till you started depressing me.'

That was the only serious thing we said all the time we were in Tenby. Then we were racing along the beach again, running into and out of the sea, splashing each other, killing ourselves laughing. Someone, an old bloke with a knotted handkerchief on his head, called us a pair of city louts, and that made us laugh more. Us, city louts. When we finished horsing around we walked back along the beach. As we got close to that bloke again we put on very posh accents and started talking loudly about the stock market. Plank said, 'Well, actually no, old chap. Dropped best part of a million. Get it back next week though, wouldn't you think?'

'Indisputably.'

And we were off again, racing and chasing and laughing like we hadn't a care in the world.

When I got back to Morecambe somebody, I honestly can't remember who, gave me a copy of the *Daily Mail*. GUARD WHO RETURNED FROM DEAD LEAVES ARMY, I saw. That was all I read – I couldn't bring myself to read any more. I was terrified at what they might have written. I got this awful feeling that they were after me again and worked myself up into a right state. A year or so later Auntie Iris told me that I'd gone to her and spent the whole night shaking and crying; but I can't remember that. All I do remember is feeling cornered again.

But there was something worse. Because of my breakdown, I suppose, the fact that they kept calling me the 'soldier back from the dead' was having a really odd affect. I knew that they didn't mean any particular harm by it. I knew they couldn't just print that some bloke called Philip Williams had done such and such because my actual name wouldn't mean anything to anyone, and who the hell would want to read an article about someone they'd never heard of? I knew that the coming back from the dead bit *made* the headline. I knew *all* that, but it still didn't help. There were times when I began to feel that I *had* been dead, and that the poor sod now walking round as Phil Williams was someone other than the Phil Williams who had died. I know that sounds crazy, but it really played on my mind, and sometimes I thought I could even remember what the original Philip Williams was like – and he was nothing like me at all. He wasn't handsomer or richer or nicer or smarter or anything like that, he just saw things differently, and could deal with his problems without panicking. He wasn't afraid of anything since he had nothing to be afraid of.

It got so bad that one evening, in a pub, I just walked up to this bloke, and asked, 'Do you know who I am?'

He was just an ordinary working chap, having a beer on his way home, I expect, so you can imagine he was a bit startled to have this lunatic coming up to him with a question like that when all he wanted was a bit of peace and quiet. He looked at me, and said, 'No.'

'I'm Philip Williams,' I told him.

'Oh. So?'

'The *real* Philip Williams.'

'Good for you,' he said, not meaning anything and turned away.

But for some reason I took it that he was taking the piss. 'Fuck you too,' I told him.

He belted me one.

I kicked him.

Some of his mates and the barman then picked me up and threw me out of the pub on my ear.

If you're ever in Morecambe and want a bit of a laugh, go into the church. One of the churches. I can't remember which one so you'll have to hunt about a bit. Just inside the door at the back there's a little dark corner where they store the prayerbooks. There's a small bench there. On it, in felt pen, you'll find:

PW + 1

PW − 1

PW = 0

Unless they've wiped me away.

You'd think that after all the moaning I'd been doing about wanting to be left alone that I'd be happy enough now, alone in my little flat. But I wasn't. I suppose it was the difference between being alone and being lonely. Or maybe it was because I *had* to be alone: ordinary people didn't want to know me, either because they believed all the crap that had been written, or else because they were scared of being sucked into all the godawful mess. And the people who *did* want to seek me out were doing it for their own reasons. Usually pressmen looking for a different angle to keep the story going. And, you know, it really was just a story to them. I wasn't real, or so it seemed.

I started getting nervous about going out again, and usually I'd wait until it was dark. I was letting myself get into a bit of a mess physically too. I'd been very fit, and now all my muscles were getting quite flabby, and I was putting on too much weight. And I did all sorts of crazy things to try and change my appearance. I grew a beard and then shaved it off. I had my head shaved too, but couldn't wait for the stuff to grow again since my head had these crazy bumps and hollows on it, and I looked like something that had been dug out of a tomb. So then I let my hair grow and grow until it was down to my shoulders, and started dressing really sloppy, letting my jeans get really dirty and torn, and wearing T-shirts with all sorts of daft slogans on them like, DEAD KENNEDYS — TOO DRUNK TO FUCK. I think I might have been doing this because it was just the opposite to the way I'd been forced to behave in the army, but I didn't actually sit down and think of it in that way. To tell the truth, I didn't know what I was trying to do. And I didn't know what I wanted, either. The only thing I knew how to do was be a soldier, and that didn't help me much now.

TWENTY-TWO

I must have been asked now a hundred times at least what made me take to drugs. Hard drugs, I mean. Not pot. Lots of the guardsmen have the odd puff of that now and again, although I expect that would be officially denied. Well, for once, I can't blame the Army. Or my family. Or my friends. Or my enemies, for that matter. The reason I went on hard drugs is very simple: *I* wanted to.

I keep hearing junkies on the telly saying that they started on the needle because they were depressed, or couldn't get a job, or came from deprived homes, or just couldn't cope with society, and I suppose that could be true enough for them. It was nothing like that with me, though. Sure I was depressed, but I didn't gape at myself in the mirror and say, 'Hey, laddie, you're depressed, why don't you go and have a fix and cheer yourself up?' I think you'd have to be a right nutter to do something like that. If I *did* have a reason other than just wanting to, it might have been that I knew hard drugs could kill you, and at that time dying wouldn't have worried me all that much. I don't think I was suicidal or anything –

I mean I wasn't deliberately setting out to top myself, but I suppose I was thinking that if it did happen, so what? Who'd care? Not me, that's for sure. And sometimes, just for a minute or two, *that* used to get me down, thinking that if I died nobody on earth would give a damn. I'd been put through all that shit, and been driven half mental, and all that would happen if I died would be everyone heaving a great sigh of relief. Some thought that is.

Anyway, what I'm trying to say is that if there were any what they call 'psychological reasons', I didn't know about them. I just thought it would be a bit of crack — if you'll excuse the pun.

If there *was* one thing, it was this: I'd been going with this girl on and off. Christine, a student teacher. She had this summer job behind a bar on the seafront. We got on pretty well, all things considered. She liked to think she was protecting me, mothering me really, which was, I suppose, what I wanted at the time. Anyway, towards the end of August, just before my birthday, she told me she had to go back to Cheshire for a while to see her parents. She came back three weeks later. To celebrate we got a bit pissed, and then she let me have it. She hadn't been to see her parents at all but had been pregnant, and had been off to have the birth terminated. Jesus, I was furious — not so much because she'd had the bloody abortion, but because she hadn't told me first. It made me feel really ashamed that I hadn't been able to comfort her when she needed it, and I felt guilty about the baby being killed off too.

It spoiled everything between us. We saw each other a couple of times, but it wasn't the same. So pretty soon I was on my own again. One night, feeling really pissed off, I told Plank about it. Being Plank, he was pretty philosophical, telling me there was no point in *my* getting down about it, since I hadn't been let in on the news. But even now I blame myself, and can't help wondering what that little baby might have been like.

It was while I was still brooding over this that I started on drugs. And to make matters worse I'd run out of money and had had to give up my flat. For a while I dossed down in the rooms of people I'd got to know, people a bit like me who'd got lost somewhere in the system and were doing the best they could to stay alive. They were the only ones who would have anything to do with me. I can see now they were, like myself, pretty messed up, and most of them, all of them in fact, were on hard drugs – not usually heroin, but speed and LSD and stuff like that.

I don't suppose you'd have thought of Morecambe as a thriving drug centre. I mean, it's not exactly the Khyber Pass, is it? But you can get just about anything you want there. Come to think of it, you can get what you want anywhere, if you know where to look for it.

One evening I was looking to buy a bit of grass. That's all I'd ever used up until then. I'd been offered all sorts of other things but had always turned them down. *I* wasn't going to screw myself up, was I? Anyway, that evening I bumped into this bloke called Gary, a small-time dealer, who was just selling enough to be able to keep a bit for himself. 'Any grass, Gary?' I asked.

'Uh-huh. Got some speed though.'

'Shit, no.'

'It's all I've got.'

'Naw.'

'Good for what ails you, man,' he told me, using the word 'man' like he'd seen it in too many bad movies. 'Shouldn't knock it till you've tried it,' he added.

And, of course, I tried it. It was quite like those drugs they used to give me in Woolwich to make me sleep, only this had the opposite effect. I stayed awake for three days and nights, tripping. And fuck, did I trip! Anyone looking at me would have taken me for some sort of zombie since I went about with this glazed look on my face and bumped into things like I thought they weren't there or that I could go through them. But my mind was really racing, picking things from my past and zooming in on them, making me focus on them, study them. The trouble was that since I wasn't in control of my mind myself, things got pretty warped. Like:

I was sitting on a bench, or maybe it was a low wall, in the centre of Morecambe. Shoppers were hurrying past. Mothers with children. Old people with dogs on leads. Pretty girls in summer dresses, their arms linked. Then a soldier went past, carrying a plastic shopping bag. My mind made my eyes fix on him. He was walking slowly away from me, his back towards me, swinging the bag a bit. He had no stripes. But as I stared at him these three stripes appeared on his arm as clear as anything. The bag became an Argie helmet with half a head in it, and it was half of old Pete's head. And all of a sudden I was running over to him and falling on my knees in front of him asking him to forgive me for kicking him when he was dead. Or thought I was. I wasn't, though. I was still sitting there, watching him disappear.

Or:

I was in the butcher's shop getting some chicken pieces. There were carcasses hanging on hooks, headless and skinned. And as I was waiting to be served those carcasses started moving, swinging back and forth like some morbid chorus line, and then twisting themselves into the shapes I'd seen the sheep on the Falklands in after they'd been blown up. I can tell you I was out of that shop pretty damn quick.

Or:

I've told you how I love little kids. Well, one morning I was just hanging about, and there was this baby in a pram crying its eyes out while its mother was in a shop buying stuff. That crying really hurt me. I kept thinking that's *me* crying; so naturally I wanted to stop it, to comfort the baby, comfort myself too. The next thing I knew I had the baby in my arms, jigging it up and down, telling the little mite not to worry, that things were never as bad as they seemed. Then the mother came out of the shop. I suppose she thought I was molesting her child, or trying to run off with it. She dropped what she'd bought – a pot of jam, I think. It smashed on the pavement and the red messy contents splattered everywhere. I thought, 'Fuck, grenade,' and started to trot off, taking, as I thought, the baby to safety. The mother started screaming like mad. She caught up with me easily enough, and grabbed her child, still shouting terrible things at me. I remember I kept saying, 'It's all right. It's all right,' but she sure as hell didn't think so. She had the baby under one arm and was hanging on to me with her free hand, yelling for the police. Luckily for me, the great British public thought *she* was the crazy one and ignored her, giving her looks that said she ought to be ashamed of herself for making such a scene. So I was able to slink away feeling a right prat.

Lack of sleep, and bad and irregular eating brought my ulcers back again, and I was pretty sick for a week or so, vomiting a lot. But I kept on taking speed and acid like a fool. When I picked up my benefits I'd buy as much as I could and sell some off, making a bit of profit and paying for my own. Nothing else seemed to matter as long as I could satisfy my yearning. I was really scruffy by now, and pretty dirty. I didn't think about things like clothes and washing. They're not the sort of things that preoccupy your mind when you're high.

I was lucky in one way: I wasn't so far gone that I couldn't realise I was getting in pretty deep, and that soon I'd be resorting to the methods a lot of people did to obtain the money for my habit – burglary and mugging and hold-ups. I was doing about an ounce of speed a week and thirty or forty Temazepam, so it was quite expensive. Anyway, one evening about six months after I'd started on those drugs, I thought, 'Shit, that's fucking awful, mugging some poor bastard and taking the money he needs to feed his wife and kids.' So I decided to set out on my own, to get away for a bit, sort of hoping that by getting away from other users I might just stop wanting the stuff myself. The trouble was I'd really got no place to go. I couldn't go home. Well, I could have gone home, I suppose, but I didn't want to have to put up with all the nagging I knew I'd get, and I was pretty ashamed of the way I looked, too. I was even beginning to be able to smell myself, which is saying something. So I decided to find myself somewhere to squat. Which isn't as hard to do as you might think. There was this big caravan park just on the outskirts of Morecambe and, since it was winter now, most of the caravans were empty. I chose a nice one and moved in.

I was coming back one day from picking magic mushrooms. I'd eaten quite a few and was pretty gone, feeling a bit silly and light-hearted. Near the caravan site I met this girl. She was lovely, very small with big brown eyes and pretty little hands. I started chatting to her, and managed to persuade her to come into the caravan with me. I wanted sex with her badly, and I was pretty crude about it. That's one things drugs do to your personality. They make you very self-centred, very selfish, very insensitive. I think I must have frightened her badly since she ran out of the caravan, looking really scared.

I don't know if she said something or if it was just a coincidence, but a couple of days later the police came and arrested me for trespassing. Funnily enough I couldn't have cared less. I wasn't in the least worried about what might happen, probably because I was in the frame of mind of thinking that nothing could be much worse than what I was going through already. I was even hoping they'd keep me inside for a while, but they didn't. Just charged me and told me what day to be in court, and then told me to piss off. So, when the day for my court appearance came, I trotted along, looking even scruffier than before, since I'd been sleeping outside, under hedges or in haybarns and things.

There were loads of us waiting to be sentenced, but everyone was in good humour. All regulars, I guess. Mostly prostitutes and people getting done for possession, or shoplifting. They all seemed to know each other anyway, and we joked about what we were up for. One woman thought it was very funny my being up for trespassing. When she stopped laughing she gave me her address and told me not to be so stupid sleeping out in the cold when there was plenty of room on the floor in her house. I said, 'Thanks very much. I might just take you up on that.'

'Do if you want. It's no big deal. The bit there is of you won't take up much space.'

'Thanks.'

'You're welcome.'

I thought that was very generous of her.

The magistrate got through us at a clipping rate, giving everyone a little sermon before fining them, or having them locked up for a few days, doing his bit towards our rehabilitation, I suppose. Came my turn and he said something about my pulling my socks up. So I did. I bent down and pulled up my frigging socks. That got a bit of a cheer from the back of the court, but the magistrate wasn't about to find it funny. He went quite red in the face and told me not to be impertinent. He also told me the court was no place for such 'levity', and slapped a £200 fine on me.

'Thanks a bunch,' I told him, and meant it. I figured I'd got off pretty light, what with all the rent I hadn't paid. Another thing that *really* pleased me: my appearance seemed to save me for once. There were a couple of reporters in the court, just local ones, and they didn't pick up on who I was. Stupid bastards, they could probably have made themselves a packet if they'd been awake and passed on the information to the nationals. *They'd* have had a field day. SOLDIER BACK FROM THE DEAD IN COURT FOR TRESPASSING, I guess they'd have said, although, knowing them, they'd have made trespassing into breaking and entering just to spice things up. Anyway, they missed out, and I felt terrific about it.

I was beginning to enjoy sleeping out of doors. It's much quieter outside than you'd think. Houses make a lot of noise during the night. But when it started getting really cold I'd visit the woman who'd given me her address at the court. She was part of a commune, I discovered, and there were dozens of people living in the house. They were all a bit weird. Very nice, but a little weird. All much older than me, mostly late thirties or early forties, and still hanging on to the sixties' hippy bit, like flower power hadn't been able to escape from Morecambe yet. Indian gurus were in favour too, and there were pictures of them on the walls, with incense burning in front of them.

Mostly we just sat in her front room and smoked pot or took a bit of speed, listening to someone playing the guitar or singing, or just talking. At least they talked. I listened. Much of the time I didn't know what they were talking about. I didn't know who the hell Jack Kerouac was, and he seemed to be a sort of guiding light for this bunch. Bob Dylan too. They played his records endlessly. Only his early ones though, before he copped out, they said, whatever that was supposed to mean. Some were into Woody Guthrie, and that always caused a bit of hassle, the others calling Guthrie shit. I didn't care one way or the other so long as they left me in peace. Actually, for some reason I found it all quite sad. I know it was a stupid sort of logic, but while I thought it was okay for *me* to mope about doing nothing because I was young, for them, nearly forty, twenty years older than me, it was kind of pathetic. Like they were all trying to hang on to their youth, but only looked and sounded sad. One of the blokes was gay, and he put it like this: 'The trouble with us, kids, is that it's our *ideas* that are mutton dressed as lamb'. Mind you, he was stoned when he said it, we all were, otherwise they'd probably have murdered him for pointing out the truth.

He was okay, that gay bloke, whatever his name was.

We got on really well. And I don't mean sex. I mean talking. I don't really think he was into sex, or maybe just dreaming about it. He always came and sat next to me on my visits. He told me, maybe when I'd given him a funny look, 'I like to sit beside pretty people,' so I guess he found me pretty. Maybe he needed glasses too. It used to make me laugh to myself just thinking that there I was chatting away happily to this bloke when only a year or so earlier I'd probably have beaten the shit out of him for daring to even look at me.

TWENTY-THREE

I hate having to tell this next bit. Not because I don't want you to know, but because I really feel bad just remembering it all.

To begin with I started needing more and more fixes to satisfy my craving. The trouble was that I didn't have the sense to take just what I needed. I started shovelling the damn stuff in — anything I could get, even heroin once or twice, but mostly speed and barbiturates — only feeling normal when I was numb. I kept kidding myself that I was doing this so I'd forget about the Falklands and all, but really I know I was doing it because I was so scared of not knowing what was going to become of me. I don't mind admitting that some days I'd do nothing but sit by myself and cry like a baby, and I remember telling myself over and over that nobody wanted me and that I was alone, and going rapidly downhill. Then my ulcers began to start playing up again. Hardly surprising, really. I honestly thought I was going to die, and that didn't please me any. I asked if I could move into the house, move in properly, until I got better, and the woman said, 'Sure, stay as long as you like.' So in I moved. I know they were all worried about my condition and they gave me this little room to myself, and left me in peace, just bringing me food now and again, but leaving me to myself. How does that famous book start? It was the best of times, it was the worst of times? Something like that. Well, it was certainly the worst of times for me. I had nightmares the like of which I couldn't have imagined. Real shockers that used to leave me sweating and shaking and wondering what the hell had hit me, and if now I really was going out of my mind. Even when I was awake I'd have hallucinations, seeing things in that room which couldn't have been there, not even *real* things, shapes of things more like.

After about two weeks of this I began to get better. The ulcers calmed down, so physically I wasn't in much pain. After all that time alone in the room it was a bit strange going downstairs again, but nobody took much notice: it was just as if I hadn't been sick at all really. I started doing chores about the house, cooking, which I'm a dab hand at, even if I say so myself. In fact it was only when I cooked that we ate anything proper, otherwise it was soup or fast food – curries and Chinese.

The best thing about the house was that everyone was so calm. There was never any hassle. Everyone did what they wanted and nobody else gave a shit. I could take my drugs in peace without having to slink around the smelly pubs or go to drug parties that seemed to take place everywhere, quite often ending up in a knifing and the police being called in. Mind you, the house itself was a bit of a mess. It never got cleaned or anything, but that didn't seem important. To tell the truth it was a right tip, with old food cartons left lying around for weeks, and clothes discarded and left lying anywhere. But it was a haven for me, and that was all that mattered. Nobody but those people would have taken me in when I needed a roof over my head, and the great thing was that they didn't give a shit who I was or what I'd done. I was Phil, and that was that.

The occupants changed quite often. People drifted off and others arrived from nowhere to take their place. Sometimes a postcard would arrive from Katmandu or Sri Lanka or Glasgow, and we'd sit for hours talking about the persons who had sent them, remembering the mad things they'd done, or what they'd said. It was like getting a card from a member of your family.

One of the occupants of the house was a young woman with two children – little girls, one aged two, the other four months. Her husband only lived across the town. They couldn't get on together at all. Sometimes he would come to see her and try to persuade her to come home with the kids, but she didn't want to, and it always ended up with them screaming at each other and fighting. Then he'd stomp off, slamming the front door behind him.

Like the rest of us the woman smoked pot and took acid, and she was heavily into meditation. She'd sit there, usually cross-legged on the floor, miles away, while the two kids yelled their heads off, not seeming to hear them at all. Usually someone else, sometimes me, would pick up the children and cuddle them, quietening them down. At first I used to get angry with her for ignoring the small things, but after a bit I began to understand what she was up to. I got a bit like her myself, setting up my own little world in my mind, and pulling myself into it, feeling safe in there and ignoring everything that went on around me. It was the only way I seemed to be able to forget how confused and lost I felt. I could imagine anything nice I wanted, and I did just that, like sitting on the bank of the Lune fishing, and quite often I really would think I *was* there, as if somehow I had transported myself to the river without moving.

Anyway, one Friday the woman came up to me and said, 'Phil, do us a big favour, will you?'

I was pretty high at the time, but I said, 'What?'

'Tell me that you'll do it first.'

'Okay. I'll do it.'

'Promise?'

'Yeah, I promise. What is it?'

'Look after the kids for me until Monday.'

I didn't know what day it was, or how long it was until Monday, but it seemed a reasonable enough request, so I smiled stupidly and agreed. The next thing I knew was that she was gone and there I was with two little girls to look after. I wasn't worried. I didn't really even think about it. I was so high I just curled up where I was and fell asleep.

The next morning was a different matter. I felt really rough. All I had was a bit of pot, and not much of that. I smoked about half and felt better. I fed the kids and cleaned them up. I quite enjoyed doing that. They were so pleased to get a bit of attention, even mine, that they giggled and laughed, and that made me giggle and laugh too. When they'd eaten I put them in the front room to play, and smoked the bit of pot I had left, watching them. I started thinking they were the two kids I'd thought I'd seen in the croft on the Falklands even though they were both girls. That started me crying again, and one of the kids came over and wiped the tears away, or tried to, and that made me cry even more.

By the afternoon I was getting jittery. I got this pain in my chest so I knew I needed something stronger than pot. But I didn't have anything. To try and take my mind off it I prepared more food for the girls and fed them, making a mess of it, dropping things and knocking things over since I couldn't keep any part of my body steady. By the time they'd finished I was really shaking, trying to think where I could get a bit of speed or smack or anything. I settled the kids down in the bedroom and started ransacking the house to find some sort of drug. I went through all my clothes, and tried all my usual hiding places. All I ended up finding was an acid tab. I swallowed that. It did nothing for me. I was really bouncing around. One of the kids started to cry so I went upstairs again to see what was wrong. I'd just got there when someone banged on the front door. So down I raced again. It was this bloke I knew. He looked as if he was going to come in, but changed his mind when he saw the state I was in. He did ask if he could bring me anything, though. I told him I could really murder some speed, and gave him some cash to get it. He said he'd get back as quick as he could.

The kids were still crying, so I went upstairs again. I don't know whether the running up and down the stairs had anything to do with it, but when I opened the door of the bedroom the strangest things started to happen. To begin with I felt icy cold. Then there was the sound of cars being driven really fast and suddenly screeching to a halt. The walls started to move in on me. And the furniture – the furniture seemed to get a life of its own and came towards me, and as it came forward it changed into cartoon beasts, only there was nothing funny about them. And you know those big glass balls that sometimes hang from the ceilings of dance halls, the ones that flash coloured lights? Well, it was as if there was one of them in the bedroom too, only as well as lights I would have sworn it was giving off some sort of poisonous gas. Anyway, I went berserk. I started fighting with the furniture, hurling it away from me, smashing everything that came within my reach. All the time I could hear myself screaming. I wanted to stop screaming but I couldn't. I wanted to stop breaking the place up but couldn't. Every time I threw a chair out of the way it got up and came back at me again. Jesus, it really was frightening.

I don't know how long it went on for, but sometime later I found myself outside the room, and literally falling down the stairs. I remember just lying there, shaking, and I stayed there for the rest of the day.

In the evening the bloke came back with the promised speed. After I'd taken some I felt much better. At least I stopped shaking like I was demented. I began to think that the whole episode had been a bad dream, but when I made some food and took it upstairs to the kids I found it had actually happened. Fuck me, you'd have thought a frigging cyclone had hit the room. I don't think there was one piece of furniture that hadn't been damaged, and the door was swinging on one hinge. The window was broken and the curtains were torn to shreds. Even some of the wallpaper had been ripped off. I just stared and stared.

I couldn't *believe* I'd done all that. But I had.

The children seemed okay, though. To tell the truth I was still in such a state that I didn't really examine them all that much. It had never dawned on me that they might be hurt. I just fed them, cleaned them, and put them to bed in another room. The next morning their Mum came home.

I was high by then, but not so high that I couldn't sense something was wrong. The woman collected the two girls and went out, giving me a dirty look as she went out. I couldn't make head nor tail of it. I thought I'd done a pretty good job with them. In fact I was quite hurt that the bitch hadn't even bothered to thank me.

A couple of hours later the police were there. Two plain clothes cops. I didn't know what the fuck they wanted. One said, 'Come on now, Phil. You're really in a mess this time. Just help us all you can, and we'll see if we can't get you some help in return.' That seemed reasonable enough, so I said, 'Okay.' I wasn't in any state to put up much resistance anyway. The drugs were beginning to wear off and I had a headache like I'd never had before. They drove me down to the cop shop.

I'm sure they must have told me why I'd been arrested, but I don't remember them doing it. I do remember them saying something about the house having been under observation for some time, and that it had been marked by the Social Services, whatever that meant. None of it made any difference to me. They could have charged me with murder and I'd have agreed just to get them off my back. All I wanted was some speed to stop me jittering and jumping about the place. In the end they read out this statement they'd written and asked me if I agreed with it. 'Yeah, yeah, yeah,' I said, and signed it. Christ alone knows what was written on it. Then they banged me up in a cell, and things got worse. I really freaked out. It was so bad they had to call a doctor in the middle of the night to give me a sedative just to shut me up.

The next thing I knew I was being sent to the famous Risley Remand Centre to wait for my trial to come up. I was kept there for three weeks, and I can tell you that I learned how battery chickens must feel. Fucking awful, that's how. I was kept in this cell with just a bed. Nothing else. If I wanted to go to the toilet I had to call someone and be escorted. Really nice that was. Since they thought I was probably suicidal, and since, anyway, I was supposed to be under observation for a psychiatric report for the court, I was in a cell by myself, which was lucky. That way I was able to keep myself out of trouble and not get mixed up in all the hassle that was going on. It seemed to me that everyone in there was as freaked out as myself, and most of them weren't on drugs of any kind. It was the not knowing what was going to happen that made everyone nervous and jumpy. They kept imagining the worst, and being locked up with people they didn't know couldn't have helped.

The screws were reasonably okay, but they couldn't cope. You could feel the whole place seething, just waiting to explode; and every day there'd be fights about nothing, just someone saying the wrong word at the wrong time would set things off, or someone knocking over someone else's tea, or accidentally bumping into someone – any excuse was enough to start a fight.

Myself I just huddled on my bunk, wishing to God I could get my hands on a bit of speed or pot. There was plenty of it available but I didn't have any cash to buy it, and I wasn't about to sell my bum even for that. Could have done though, there was a lot of that going on there, too.

I don't know if the psychiatric report ever found its way to the court, but if it did it must have been a gas. I never saw a doctor all the time I was in Risley, let alone a shrink. Maybe they'd got a standard form for nutters that they just sign. Wouldn't surprise me. In fact, the only stranger I did see was a solicitor from Manchester. He told me I was being charged with two counts of assault which really confused me since I couldn't remember assaulting anyone. He also said he wouldn't be representing me, and when I asked him what the fuck he was doing there then, he told me I would be having legal aid and that he'd be sending his 'findings' to the appropriate quarter. *I* never found out what *he* found out. I don't know if anyone did.

Anyway, somehow I got through my three weeks' remand, and one morning I was handcuffed to a policeman and carted off to court in Morecambe. I looked a right mess by now, and I could see the judge giving me his disdainful eye. Not that I blame him – a drugged out, scruffy freak ain't a pretty sight. I stood there like a right prat while loads of people did their act. The police read out the charge: causing actual bodily harm to the two little girls. Apparently they'd been hit by some of the flying furniture, but luckily they hadn't been injured seriously in any way. Then someone else got up and had a few words to say. Then another bloke, whom now I suppose was my solicitor, although I'd never seen him before, waffled away for a while. I was standing there feeling really dizzy and stupid, and saying to myself, 'This is fucking daft. They can't be talking about me.' But they were. A social worker whom I'd never met either was saying that under the circumstances I should be given probation; the circumstances being, I think, that I was dependent on drugs and that the assault had been an accident. I was petrified they were going to bring up the whole Falklands bit again, using it to make me out as cracked, but nobody mentioned that luckily. That would really have made me go berserk, I think.

When they'd all finished the magistrates went off for

a little chat. Actually they were gone for quite a while, and when they came back the head one gave me a talking to. He explained how serious the charges were, and that while he appreciated that there were extenuating circumstances and a case of diminished responsibility, he simply could not have people like me going about doing the things I'd done and getting away with it scot-free. However, out of the kindness of his heart he was going to refrain from imposing what he called the 'full weight of the law'. He gave me eight weeks on each count, and said he hoped I appreciated how lenient he'd been. And that was that.

There's been loads of books written about life in prison so I'm not going to give my version. It's just about the same for everyone, and anyway, if you've never actually done time it always sounds phoney, and a bit like it's all made up by some ex-con trying to get some sympathy. So I'll get through it as quickly as possible.

After the court I was taken immediately to Walton, near Liverpool. I was there a week while they made up their minds where to send me next. It was quite a good week really since my cell mates were a couple of buskers in for nonpayment of fines, and they kept me laughing with the crazy stories they told. Like the time they were really stoned out of their minds and the bloke with the fiddle kept playing the wrong notes, making a right hash of some well-known concerto or something. They were outside a cinema and someone left the queue to tell them to stop mutilating poor old Mozart or Beethoven or whoever it was supposed to be. Anyway, they ended up convincing this know-all that it was being played properly since it was this new variation by some Polish guy, and they got a fiver from him for their trouble. Just shows you how dumb some people who think they know everything can really be.

From Walton they sent me by coach with a load of other deadly criminals to the Hindley Youth Custody Centre, near Wigan. I was only there for about nine weeks since I got one-third remission for good behaviour, and they knocked off the time I'd been on remand too. I spent most of the time doing cleaning jobs about the place, and the highlight of my stay was the day I had a tooth pulled out by the prison dentist.

Before I knew it my time was up. They gave me about thirty quid and a rail ticket back to Lancaster.

Oh, yeah. One other thing. There'd been a reporter in the court, and he made a name for himself. He wrote this really crappy article about me under the headline FALLEN HERO, having the time of his life telling all his dumb readers all about my drug addiction, and the way I was living, and the terrible fall I'd made in society.

Anyway, I'm glad that bit's over and done with. I don't even like thinking about it any more.

TWENTY-FOUR

It was quite strange being on the outside again. I hadn't had any drugs for a while, and I was seeing things a bit straighter. I think everything would have been all right if I'd been left alone to sort myself out in my own time, but I wasn't.

I'd only been home a couple of days when suddenly the press were crawling all over the place again. They'd started making the film *Tumbledown* and it was causing a bit of a stir, so the press came to Halton to see what I had to say about it. They tried every angle to link me in, one of them even asking me, 'Isn't it true that you were one of the stretcher-bearers who carried Lawrence off Tumbledown?'

'No,' I said. Maybe I was. I didn't fucking know. I mean, when you're lugging some poor sod off the side of a mountain your brain isn't figuring out that here's film material and you'd better remember the details for posterity. And even if I did know, I wasn't about to tell those shits.

'We heard you were,' he said.

'Well, you heard wrong then, didn't you?'

They weren't too happy with that. A bloke from one of the main tabloids even threatened to do a big spread about my court case and conviction if I didn't give him an exclusive interview. I told him where he could shove his paper. What he didn't know was that by now I didn't give a shit what they printed about me. Nothing they did now could be worse than what they'd already done to me and my family. It was a really good feeling when I realised that. I was able to tell them just what I thought of them and their scummy papers, and not worry that they might be unkind to me.

Anyway, when they saw I wasn't about to give them any spicy crap they pissed off, probably to lay siege on some other poor bastard.

I was pretty surprised when I got a letter from a thing called St Pancras Films saying they wanted to make a film about me and my experiences. I thought someone was having me on at first. But it was true enough, and I was daft enough to feel quite pleased, thinking that maybe *my* side of things were about to be told at last. They started off by saying they wanted my permission to do it, but it wasn't long before they made it clear that they were going ahead whether I agreed or not.

I said okay.

It was quite interesting really, seeing them make it. A bloke called Paul Greengrass was the producer, and Tom Bell played my Dad, Rita Tushingham my Mam, and

David Thewlis me, and all of a sudden there I was hobnobbing with the frigging stars.

I didn't receive any money for the film, although they paid my fare to the set a couple of times and gave me a couple of lunches, but that was it. People keep telling me I was crazy not to have made something out of it, but I didn't.

The film was called *Resurrected* which they all seemed very pleased with. But in the front of the script they sent us there's this:

The idea for this script arose out of Guardsman Philip Williams's experience in the 1982 Falklands War and its aftermath. While true to the spirit of that experience, dramatic licence has been taken and the script is not intended to be a faithful representation of the events that happened or the characters involved.

I think they were just riding on the back of the Falklands euphoria, and hoping their film would get the same publicity *Tumbledown* did, having a right go at the Army, and the Scots Guards in particular, without bothering about the truth too much. They didn't seem to think that what I *had* been through was bad enough. I could just picture them sitting around a table saying, 'Shit, is that all they did to him? *That* won't make anyone talk about our film. Let's make this and that happen. Really give the Army some stick.' I think the truth of what happened to me is quite bad enough for anyone to appreciate that there are shits in the Army just like in every organisation. Besides, they didn't seem to understand that *I'd* be blamed. And I was. There was quite a fuss really. A couple of MPs started having their say, giving out about the film, calling it a dreadful slur, calling it one-sided – *my* supposed side, of course – and accusing it of denigrating the army's achievements, and Labour MP Tam Dalyell called for a public inquiry into the Army's behaviour.

Mam went to a private viewing of the film before it was released and wasn't too thrilled; she'd been hoping that at last the truth was going to be told, and was disappointed that they'd invented some scenes.

So much for my time as a star – I wouldn't want to do it again.

Still, it was an experience, and it taught me a few things, so it wasn't all a waste. Come to think of it, nothing ever is.

So then what? Well, then things started getting pretty tense and strained at home. Dad started his moaning again about my not having a job. I know he did it because he was worried about me, but I didn't want to hear all that stuff. You know what the trouble was? My Dad never really understood what everything had done to me, and I never really understood what it had done to him. We couldn't talk about it without fighting and shouting at one another. If we could have maybe things would have been okay, but we couldn't. Finally I got so fed up I left home and went to Lancaster. I found myself a nice little squat and moved in with a couple of mates. Good mates really, people who'd helped me. They were into Animal Rights and all that, so I used to give them a hand. To me it was all a bit of a lark, but they took it very seriously. Mind you, after a bit I started taking it seriously too when I saw some of the things people did to animals. Mostly we'd break into schools and colleges and release the little creatures waiting to be experimented on – rabbits and frogs and rats mostly. It was great to see them hopping away, free instead of ending up in some bottle of alcohol or whatever they pickle them in. We raided a few battery farms too, letting the chickens out. There were so many of them we could only let a few out at a time, but a few was better than none. That was really awful. The poor things couldn't walk. Didn't seem to know what their legs were for, never having used them. A couple of times we sabotaged hunts, putting down false scents, and jeering the elegant yobs as they trotted past on their horses. They used to go mad, trying to run us down with Land Rovers, or employing tricks to try and catch us. Fat chance they had of catching us. We'd go home, smoke a bit of pot, and celebrate for the fox.

I was sitting alone in the house one evening when the police came. They asked me if I knew where a bloke called Philip Williams was.

'Who?'

'Philip Williams.'

'Never heard of him.'

'We know he squats here.'

'Not here.'

'You're sure?'

'Sure I'm sure.'

I heard them saying they better try my home as they were leaving, so I knew they'd probably be back. I gathered up my bits and took off, moving to another house belonging to friends and stayed there, not going out, for a couple of weeks. Needless to say I was quite interested to know what they were looking for, and why I was of such interest. I supposed it was something to do with Animal Rights, as we'd been getting a fair bit of hassle from the police about that. I nearly shit myself when I met my brother, Gareth, in the town centre one day and he told me they wanted me for questioning about a murder. Fuck me, murder! I knew I hadn't murdered anyone, but I also knew anything can be pinned on anyone if it serves a purpose.

Anyway, after a couple of weeks they caught up with me. They were pretty angry with the way I'd tricked them before, and warned me I'd bloody well better co-operate this time or they'd get me for something, even if it wasn't murder. Well, I was stoned and the house stank like a bloody opium den, so I co-operated. They soon realised that I wasn't the person they were after, and they said, 'Well, that's you eliminated,' and left me, telling me to keep my nose clean. That experience didn't do my cardiac rating much good, and I figured maybe

I'd had enough of Lancaster, and that Lancaster'd probably had enough of me, too.

I was still trying to figure out where to go and what to do when I met Tracy.

TWENTY-FIVE

I've never been very good at forming close relationships. Even when I was a kid, long before the Falklands and all that, I used to keep myself very much to myself. Mam always said I was a watcher, not a talker, and she's right again. The way I see it is that you can learn a lot by watching, but you'll learn bugger all if you're talking all the time. Let the others yap away, and they'll soon make it clear whether they're genuine or not.

Even with Tracy I was always a bit reserved, which used to drive her mad. She was at Lancaster University when we met, and we hit it off straight away. She was alone in Lancaster. Like myself she found it pretty hard to communicate, but with each other we didn't have to try. It was like we always knew what the other one was thinking, and we saw things in much the same way. She had a little flat of her own, and after we'd known each other a while, I moved in. It was sort of as if we were married, only without all the strings. Often we'd sit and dream about what we'd like to do. It usually came down to just taking off, and wandering wherever we wanted, not tied down at all to anything or anybody. Nothing very exotic mind, not Katmandu or stuff like that. So, when Tracy finished at university, she said, 'Why don't we do it?'

'You're on,' I said, and that was that. We packed up all her stuff carefully and stored it away. We both had rucksacks and we put what clothes we thought we'd need into them. We bought a small tent, a proper one like they use when climbing Everest, and walked out of the flat.

I phoned Mam. 'Mam, I'm leaving,' I said.

'Where are you going?'

'I don't know.'

'That's stupid, Phil. You must know where you're going.'

'I don't. Anywhere,' I told her, and it dawned on me then how terrific that was. Anywhere. Any bloody place I wanted. Nobody telling me I *had* to go here or there, or be in such and such a place at such and such a time. I know it sounds really daft, but for the first time in my life I felt as though I was about to be free.

I didn't expect Mam to understand, and she didn't. Her life is very tidy and ordered and secure, and she was totally baffled by this crazy, mad son she'd produced. 'Why not come home and we'll talk about it?' she suggested.

'Can't, Mam. I'm off right now.'

'What if someone wants to get in touch with you?'

'Just tell them the truth – you don't know where I am.'

'But me, Phil. If *I* want to contact you?'

'I'll ring you now and again.'

'I don't like it, Phil – you just going off like this.'

'I know. But it's what I want right now. Don't worry, I'll be okay.'

'What am I going to tell your Dad?'

'Just tell him what I told you.'

'He won't like that, you know.'

'He won't mind. Glad to see the back of me probably.'

'That's not true, Phil, and you know it. Your Dad's always done what he thought was best for you. You never gave him a chance.'

'Okay. Whatever you say, Mam. Bye.'

I hung up. I didn't want to say any more. She was making me feel guilty again, and probably she was right to do that, but I didn't want to have any of it.

Anyway, Tracy was waiting, and I suddenly got the awful feeling that if we didn't leave immediately all the excitement would vanish, and we'd change our minds, and never get going at all.

'So, where are we going?' I asked.

Tracy giggled. 'Wherever you want.'

'South.'

'Right.'

It was June 1988. Hot and dry and really glorious and, honestly, for me, it was the greatest day ever. We made our way to the outskirts of Lancaster, and started to hitch. 'Tell you what,' Tracy said. 'Wherever the first ride we get is going to, that's where we'll go.'

'Fine.'

A lorry pulled up. 'Want a lift?'

'You bet.'

'Where you heading?'

'Any damn place.'

'Just like that, eh?'

'Just like that.'

'Wrexham any good?'

'Great.'

So that's where we went first. Wrexham.

I don't expect you to agree with the sort of life we led for the next year, but it'd be nice to think you could understand what it meant to me. No ties, no orders, no press, nothing except the open air and the freedom to go where I pleased. We went just about everywhere in England and Wales, camping out, causing no one any bother. The only sour thing was when we went to Stonehenge for the summer solstice. What should have been a joyful festival with people enjoying themselves turned into a riot because the police had been ordered to keep everyone away. The stupid thing was that none of us wanted any trouble, and the people who lived in the area were really friendly to us and very kind. Some of them even joined us in our protest against the police, one old boy giving an inspector hell, saying, '*You're* the ones causing all the trouble. Not the kids. Why don't you piss off back where you belong and let people enjoy

what's left of our heritage?' We gave him a great cheer
for that. It really seems crazy to me that lots of us had
been ready to get killed for England and now we weren't
being allowed even a look at a bit of it. And I don't mean
only me. There were blokes there who'd been injured in
Northern Ireland, as well as the Falklands, even some men
who'd fought in the Second World War – not everyone
who's called a hippy is a young layabout. We come in all
shapes and sizes, all age groups, all sorts of backgrounds;
but we're all lumped together under the same heading, and
treated like shit. Can I ask you something serious? What's
the point in having a place like Stonehenge if you're not
allowed to enjoy its wonder like you're supposed to enjoy
it? What's the point in preserving it at all if it's only kept
for tourists to stare at? Seems right bloody daft and illegal
to me. Okay, so there's some thick yobbos who might try
and vandalise the stones with stupid graffitti, but that's
the minority. That year there were about fifty thousand of
us there, and I can tell you we had more respect for the
stones and the mysteries about them than half the poxy
tourists, some of whom I heard saying, 'Is that all there is?
Just stones?' like they'd expected fucking Disney World
or something.

After Stonehenge Tracy and I tagged along with a
group which the papers have labelled the Peace Move-
ment, using that tag like it was something dirty. I wish
everyone could take a trip with them sometime. Mostly
they're really gentle people who make no demands on
anyone, just asking to be left alone to lead the quiet sort
of lives they want to lead.

We went all over the country, attending music festivals and fairs. Tracy and me even started doing craftwork, selling it at the fairs to make a few bob. What I liked best was just listening to the travellers talk. Usually in the evenings groups would gather to chat. Someone would start telling a story, and before you knew where you were, you'd find he was someone who'd had a really interesting life and who was quite happy to share his experiences with anyone who wanted to listen. And there was no such thing as 'that's mine, you can't have it'. If someone had something that they felt someone else needed more, they'd give it to them without having to be asked. Nobody had to go hungry. Nobody had to sleep without some sort of shelter. The little kids could run from trailer to trailer or tent to tent without their parents being scared out of their wits that something awful was going to happen to them.

And there were no rules. There didn't have to be. You don't go thieving and causing trouble for your friends, do you?

Come the end of August, Tracy had to go home to see her parents for a while, so I decided I'd go back up North and see mine. Mam was a bit shocked when she saw me appear looking like something the cat had dragged in, as she said. Hippies aren't all that common in Halton, you see. But I could tell she was pleased to have me home for a bit. Dad wasn't too thrilled either by the way I looked, asking me why I didn't smarten myself up and get a haircut instead of behaving like a

tramp. But he didn't kick me out, which must mean
something. I think that my being away for so long had
given us all a chance to cool down, or maybe by then
they'd given up all hope of my settling down to their
way of life.

One thing really surprised me – the way Mam took
to Giro. I haven't told you about Giro, have I? Well, she
was a little brown and white rat I'd bought. She travelled
everywhere with me, mostly inside my shirt, but often
sitting on my shoulder, gazing about her, admiring the
beauties of old England. She was great company, and
once she got me out of a bloody tricky situation. That
was in London. I'd got off the bus from Scotland on my
way back to Devon and was gasping for a bit of pot.
Naturally I found some and was just wondering where
I'd go to have a quiet smoke when these two cops came
up to me, and asked me what I thought I was doing.
They do that all the time when you look like me. I think
they just regard hippies as their natural enemies for some
reason. Anyway, they didn't seem to believe me when I
said I was waiting for a bus to Devon, and decided I
might add to their tally of arrests if they searched me.
I was scared, as they'd certainly find my bit of pot, and
that would mean more hassle and probably a few days
in the frigging slammer. But there was nothing I could
do about it. They took me to one side and started their
search. They hadn't got far when out popped old Giro,
wriggling her little pink nose. Christ, you'd have thought
she was a bloody python the way they jumped. It certainly put the damper on their desire to search further,

and they told me to piss off and stop loitering. I bought Giro a bar of KitKat for that. KitKat was her favourite. Maybe she'd been watching the telly without my knowing.

Anyway, Mam really took to her, and made a great fuss of her, although Dad thought she was dirty, and probably carried rabies.

There was a letter waiting for me from the *Sunday Times Magazine*, saying they'd like to do an article on me. I thought, shit, not again. But Mam felt it might be a good idea since, after all, the *Sunday Times* was the *Sunday Times*, wasn't it, and *they* wouldn't print a lot of bullshit. I wasn't so sure, but decided to have a go anyway.

As it turned out I needn't have worried. The reporter, Mick Brown, was straight enough and wasn't interested in writing crap. And the photographer he brought with him, Mike Abrahams, gave me a laugh or two, taking his work very seriously and posing me in artistic settings. I confess that I might have given him a bit of a rough time; I was missing Tracy, and was bloody nervous about more revelations about my life, so I got myself pretty doped up before he started taking his snaps. But just pot.

When they'd finished Mick Brown slipped me a few quid. That was the first time anyone had ever given me money for an article, despite what everyone thought. I was a bit embarrassed taking it, but you don't look a gift horse in the mouth, as they say. I don't anyway.

A funny thing is that because of that article this book came to be written, but I'll explain about that later.

Tracy phoned from home and told me her parents wanted her to stay with them for a while. I didn't like that a lot but I didn't *really* mind. She gets on well with her folks and I think it's nice for a girl to have her parents backing her up in what she does. I told her that was okay by me. I also told her that I'd be off on the road again soon but that I'd drop her a card and let her know where I was.

I waited until Dad had gone off to work before telling Mam I was leaving.

'Where to this time?' she asked.

'Don't know.'

She started shaking her head.

'Don't worry, Mam. I'm doing what I want.'

'Well, I don't understand it at all, Phil,' she said. 'But if you're happy I suppose it's all right.'

'I'm happy, Mam.'

I was even happier when I was on the road again, not knowing where I was heading, and not caring either. As it turned out I found myself in Devon. Pure chance. Pure chance too that I met some people who had a spare room in a house, and suggested that I move in for a while. I did, and really liked it. Everyone living there was on the dole, and the DHSS payed their rent direct to the landlady which suited her fine. Before I knew it I'd made the same arrangement, and it came as something of a surprise to realise that I was living in a house *legally* for the first time in years.

In February 1989 the article about me appeared in the *Sunday Times*. By that time Tracy was back with me, and it was she who spotted it. She read it first without telling me anything just in case there was any crap in it that would upset me. There wasn't. She sat on my bed and read it all again, to me this time, aloud. It was such a relief that they hadn't shafted me or torn me to pieces that we could allow ourselves a good laugh at the pictures, especially the main one which was very good although it really showed how high I'd been when it was taken . . . But it was very strange hearing Tracy read the bits about the Falklands – that had all happened seven years earlier, and here they were still writing about it, and about me, which was even odder.

And sure enough, the article brought the fruitcakes out again with their stupid letters, saying how sorry they were to hear I was still alive, and hoping that the drugs would kill me, or Aids, or hadn't I yet discovered that the best thing I could do for everyone's sake was to put a bullet through my brain? But after about a month the letters stopped coming, and I hadn't actually seen any of them anyway: Mam had taken to censoring my mail, making sure she only sent on anything that might please me.

Then, about two months later, another letter was forwarded to me, and I thought, Jesus, what does this nut want? I'd been having quite a lot of Jesus freaks writing, hoping to save my soul, and I supposed this was from another. It wasn't, though. It was just a card from a bloke in Scotland saying he'd read the article and had been shocked by what had happened to me, and he told me to cheer up and that if I was ever up his way to look in. He didn't ask any questions and didn't seem to want anything, which was a change. I nearly didn't answer it but thought that would be rude, so I wrote a short note back saying I might take him up on his offer to pay a visit. Over the next few months he wrote back, and I wrote to him a few times, and then, since I was coming up to Lancaster anyway, I arranged to go that bit further and visit him.

We got on really well. He was a lot older than me, in his fifties, but he'd been into flower power in America when he was my age and didn't seem to give a shit what I looked like, although he did tell me to take a bath since I stank pretty high. What I liked best about him was that he wasn't out to try and change me or make me feel the way I was living was wrong. What he said was, 'I don't give a toss who you are or what you've done in the past. I'll judge you as *I* find you now.' And you can't ask for fairer than that. He was a writer, so was sort of expected to have weirdo friends. I know his neighbours gave me some funny looks. He introduced me to some of his friends, painters mostly, like Jeremy and Deirdre, and it was really great to be able to chat away and not worry what they might be thinking about me.

Anyway, one evening I was waffling on about the lies

that had been told about me and someone said, 'Why don't you write your own version?'

'Oh sure.'

Maurice, the bloke I was staying with, said, 'Yes. Why not?'

'*I* can't write that sort of thing.'

'If you want to do it, I'll help you.'

'I'll think about it.'

'Do.'

So, I thought about it. For ages I'd wished I could get my side of everything across. Not making myself out to be an angel or anything, just telling the truth. But every time I'd said anything at all I'd been screwed, so I was pretty suspicious by now. But finally I said I'd give it a try.

Maurice was very strict with me. Before we started he warned me that if I was serious about it I'd have to tell everything, even the things that made me look like shit, and that he wasn't going to let me use the book to take my revenge on people who'd shafted me. He had a proper contract drawn up to make sure I'd get my royalties and things. He even got me my own agent to take care of my side of things. We had a few right old rows, though. He gave me deadlines, and bullied the hell out of me if I didn't stick to them. That was after I went to Devon. While I was in Scotland I could tell him things, but when I left I used to have to send him pages of stuff. How the poor bastard understood them I don't know. They were all mixed up as I'd just put down my thoughts as they came into my head. It was great, though, being able to tell someone everything and know that nothing was going to be twisted or changed, and that I had the right to give every goddam page the okay before it was printed. Some of it was tough going, and I had quite a few nightmares because of it. It wasn't easy remembering the Falklands and old Pete and all.

Anyway, what you've been reading is what we did.

TWENTY-SIX

Like I've said before, the thing that has confused me most is why the press should have been so obsessed by me. Okay, so maybe the fact that I'd survived for a long while by myself and supposedly come back from the dead was interesting for a bit. But, Jesus, that was ages ago, and they still keep after me. Even when Maurice and me were doing this book I had a letter from the *Sunday People* saying it wanted to do another article on me. But like I told you, I'm very posh now, with my own agent, so I sent that letter on to him. He's a right tough old bastard – actually, he's a tough young bastard – so I guess he knew what he was doing when he said to ignore it. In any case I probably would have ignored it anyway since it was signed by some John Smith, who called himself 'Man of the People', which I thought was fucking arrogant, and pretty ignorant, too.

Anyway, I'm hoping that this book will put an end to all their crap. If they write anything that's not here it's clear they're lying again.

That film I was telling you about, *Resurrected*, finally
went on release and was given a lot of publicity. Naturally the press were soon after me again, hoping I'd
give them some shit to print. It was obvious none of
them gave a damn how I might be feeling. Except old
Barry Norman, that is – when he reviewed it on his TV
programme he sounded very concerned about what effect
it might have on me, seeing everything raked up again.
That really touched me.

The local rag, the *Lancashire Evening Post*, kept
badgering my parents, and when they said they didn't
know where I was (just to keep the vultures off their
backs) this really crappy story was printed under the
headline RIDDLE OF 'MISSING' FALKLANDS WAR
SOLDIER WHO INSPIRED FILM, saying, 'Mystery
today surrounded the whereabouts of back-from-the-
dead soldier Philip Williams – just as a film based on his
life story is set to be released . . . the former soldier is
said to be unhappy with the film, which the producers
say is merely "influenced" by his story.'

Well, to begin with, there was no mystery – my parents
and all my friends knew where I was, but they weren't
about to tell some two-bit newspaper. Besides, I hadn't
even seen the film at that time, so how the shit could I
have been unhappy?

Then the *Sunday People* got in on the act. They had
the headline FALKLANDS LOST HERO DOES A RUN-
NER. I was supposed to be unhappy and upset over
the film which, they said, was made without my co-
operation. And they had this picture of me grinning

like a cat with one of David Thewlis, who played me in the film, next to it.

Eventually I did see the film. Paul Greengrass, the producer, got in touch with me and asked if I'd like to come to London for a viewing. He sent me a rail ticket and, of course, I went.

So what did I make of it? Well, I was pretty impressed, to tell the truth. The acting was really terrific and as a film it's one of the best I've ever seen. What I didn't like was that although they had based the film on my experiences it seemed to have very little to do with me. I mean, they put in so much sensational fiction that, to my mind, they changed it from being what would have been a good historical document into just another war film and, Christ knows, we've seen enough of them. I think it's a pity they did that, but there you are. Anyway, it sure as hell didn't make me unhappy, and I'm not about to string myself up out of grief.

So what now? Well, now I'm much easier in my mind, and my life is quite happy really. I've no money and no job, but not from the lack of trying, honestly. I must have applied for at least three hundred jobs in the last eighteen months and it's always the same thing: either I'm rejected because I've no experience, which is fair enough, I suppose, although how they expect me to get experience without being given a job, I don't know, or because my reputation has gone ahead of me and possible employers think because of the way I look and what I've been through, I must be some sort of fruitcake. You can see their minds ticking over, imagining me as a really disruptive element, and then saying 'Well, we'd love to give you the job, but . . .' But who knows, something may turn up, someone might decide to test my brain rather than go by what they see or what they've heard.

So, all I've got is me, and at last I honestly feel that I own myself for the first time, and it's quite a discovery to find that I don't need all the things I once thought were so important for a happy life. You can believe me that the things we think we want aren't ever the things we need to be content. Really need, I mean. Of course, it might seem to you that I've taken the easy way out, what they call 'dropping out of society' and all, but I don't believe I have. I'm certainly not ashamed of the way I live. In fact, the only thing I *am* ashamed of is that I was so bloody stupid that I allowed myself to be conned into believing that there was only *one* way to live, of accepting without question that it was normal and right to join the Army and go off with the absolute intention of killing other young blokes who'd been conned just like myself, of imagining that material success was all that mattered. You can't know what a relief it is when you discover that no one *needs* all the tatty possessions they keep slinging at us on the telly, and getting into debt and being under someone else's control just to have a fucking dishwasher or video recorder. Now, every day, I'm just grateful that I came out of all the shit alive and intact, and that I've no one to thank for that but myself.

So what does he want, you might be saying? All of us to drop out like he has, and do nothing? I'm not saying that at all. I know there are lots of good and kind people in this world who really want possessions and who are quite prepared to sacrifice a lot of things to get them. That's fine by me. If they want to live like that, why shouldn't they? All I'm saying is that everyone should be allowed to lead the sort of life they want to lead without being sneered at, or harassed, or bullied, or made to feel inferior. That's how they do it, you know. They make you feel a real failure if you don't have a flash car, and an up-market house, and all the plastic junk that goes with them. It just seems to me that I'd be a real failure if I had to depend on such things to impress people. Or to impress myself, which would be really awful. The great thing is that when you discover that all the crap they give you about success is a pack of lies you stop envying people, stop running yourself ragged trying to keep up with some person who doesn't really matter and who probably doesn't give a damn about you anyway. You start to see how pathetic it all is, in fact. All it leads to is hurt and pain, and I never want to see anyone in pain for the rest of my life.

I've got the drugs under control too, I'm pleased to say. Okay, so I do smoke pot from time to time, but the hard stuff no longer holds any appeal. All that does is make you lose control of your own mind, although I can understand why some people want it that way: other people have fucked them up so much that it seems simpler to do away with their minds altogether. Me, I've gone back to the way I used to be as a kid – not saying much to anyone, not criticising, just quietly observing and wondering how we let the world get into such a fuck-awful mess. Anyway, I'm no philosopher, and I'm no worse and no better than anyone else, so why should I try and impose my way on others?

There is one little bit of advice I'll pass on for free, though. If it ever happens that you feel the urge to be patriotic and join the Army, and if some lunatic should decide a war would be quite fun and packs you off to do their fighting for them, don't, for Christ's sake, be dumb enough to get lost. And, above all, don't come back injured. You won't fit the system if you do. They don't want injured heroes. They simply don't know what to do with them. Injured heroes are a drain on resources. Sure they'll make a fuss of you to start with, but after that you'll find they get really cheesed off with some cripple badgering them for a bit of treatment or a few quid on which to survive. It's nothing new, mind. It's always been like that. Same after every war. Just ask your dad or your grandad.

No, if you want them to love you, if you really want to be called a hero, make sure you come back dead. It's far simpler. Far tidier for everyone in the long run. And especially for yourself.

AFTERWORD

On 5 February 1989 I read an article in the *Sunday Times Magazine*, which is not a newspaper I normally purchase: that day I got it purely by chance. The article, by Mick Brown, was about the plight of Philip Williams.

To this day I do not know why I reacted as I did. I wrote to Philip. Just a card, expressing my concern and disquiet at the way he had been treated, telling him to cheer up, and saying that if he was ever passing through this area to please drop in as there would be a bed for the night and food if he needed it. I have never done such a thing before. I have never written to other writers, regardless of how much I may have enjoyed their work. I have never written to a newspaper. It is totally out of character for me to write to strangers. But write to Philip I did. And Philip wrote back.

We corresponded off and on for a couple of months and then, at my suggestion, Philip came to stay for a week.

Frankly, when I first set eyes on him, I wondered what

I had let myself in for: long hair, earrings, and jeans, more tortured than distressed, are not my scene, good conservative Irish Catholic that I am. To my shame, when we went shopping for food, I tried to slide three paces in front or three paces behind him in case we met anyone I knew. Later Philip let me know he had been aware of this but instead of being insulted as I most certainly would have been, he found it highly amusing, and was quite prepared to overlook my behaviour.

Philip is, I think, the only intrinsically gentle person I have ever met. There isn't a wicked bone in his body. He does not know the meaning of the words 'spite' or 'greed' or 'malice' or 'envy'.

He has taught me a lot.

He has been grievously hurt, mauled by the tabloid press which, by innuendo and downright lies, has, quite literally, ruined his life. He has never had the chance to explain his side of the story in full. Each time he tried he was betrayed, misquoted, sensationalised or vilified. Only the *Sunday Times* article was accurate, but that only told part of the story: by the time they approached him Philip was so battered that he was reluctant to reveal anything that had not been printed before.

The outcome of Philip's stay was an agreement that we would try and tell his true story. It was not a decision taken lightly by either of us. He had to trust me, and I am flattered that he did. I had never attempted anything but fiction, and was not at all sure that I could adapt to writing fact. But, as Philip said, 'Let's try anyway.' So we tried, and this book is the result of our attempt.

It took a supreme effort on Philip's part to recount all the harrowing details again. Putting them into the written word, I hope I have not let him down.

M. S. Power